John

From Sal. Xmas 1961.

MODERN RAILWAYS THE WORLD OVER

A luxury U.S. trans-Continental streamliner – the Great
Northern Railway's diesel-hauled 'Empire Builder'
between Chicago and the Pacific coast, photographed
below the peaks of Glacier National Park during its
crossing of the spectacular Montana Rocky Mountains.
This train is described in greater detail in Chapter 4.

[*Great Northern Railway*

MODERN RAILWAYS
the world over

G. FREEMAN ALLEN

A Dutch-Swiss 'Trans-Europe Express' diesel train.
[*Y. Broncard*

LONDON:

Ian Allan Ltd

Contents

The world rail speed record-holders – French National Railways electric locomotives Nos. CC-7107 and BB-9004, each of which attained a maximum speed of 205½ m.p.h. during tests in March, 1955.

[French Railways

Acknowledgments

Author and publishers express their gratitude to the Locomotive & Allied Manufacturers Association, the English Electric Co. and Messrs J. Stone & Co. (Deptford) for the loan of colour blocks acknowledged to them, and to the various manufacturers, railway systems and private individuals who have supplied the illustrations credited to them.

Published by Ian Allan Ltd., Hampton Court, Surrey and printed in the United Kingdom by Cox & Wyman Ltd., London, Fakenham and Reading.

1

STEAM'S ELEVENTH HOUR

IN the spring of 1959 a British railway enthusiast society, with the co-operation of the Eastern Region of British Railways, marked fifty years of its existence with one of the fastest railruns recorded in this country. Hauling an 8-coach, 295-ton special train chartered by the society, Class 'A4' 4–6–2 No. 60007 *Sir Nigel Gresley* was whipped up to a maximum speed of 112 m.p.h. on the 1 in 178 to 200 descent of Stoke bank, between Grantham and Peterborough – indeed, had those on the Pacific's footplate not decided that acceleration had gone far enough and eased *Sir Nigel* down, the pace would almost certainly have risen to somewhere between 115 and 120 m.p.h. before the bank levelled off and the speed-restricted curves of Peterborough got too near. Moreover, this was not the only 'century' scored by No. 60007 that day; on the outward run from London in the morning 101 m.p.h. had been notched down the hill beyond Hitchin and at a later stage of the return trip a further 100 m.p.h. was recorded after Huntingdon – this last on a stretch scarcely more favourable to high speed than level track, and one over which nothing approaching a three-figure speed had ever before been experienced.

Here was a nominally 22-year-old machine (nominally, because many major parts of a steam locomotive, such as the boiler, are renewed during its career) built to a design of 1935, showing it was capable of the highest speeds likely to be operated in regular railway service in the third quarter of the twentieth century, without overheating or any other mechanical trouble. In the same year, across the Atlantic, steam power was still entrusted with some of the heaviest loads regularly operated anywhere in the world. On the Duluth, Missabe & Iron Range Railway of the U.S.A. huge 2–8–8–4 articulated locomotives, 127ft 8in long over engine and tender and weighing 569 tons with a full tender-load of 26 tons of coal and 25,000 gallons of water, were shouting to the skies as they set 200-wagon, 18,000-ton trains of iron ore on the move from the mines of Minnesota to the shores of Lake Superior.

Yet, as this book is being written, the Gresley 'A4' Pacifics are facing replacement by 3,300 h.p. diesel locomotives on their most important express jobs. And had you visited the Duluth, Missabe & Iron Range during the 1959 or 1960 winter you would have found the 2–8–8–4s cold in store. The D.M. & I.R., like almost every other U.S. railroad, has on its books sufficient diesel locomotives to handle its normal traffic and is one of the very few U.S. systems to maintain a small reserve of steam power only to cope with extra trains at seasonal periods of peak loading. On most of the world's major railways steam power is either declining rapidly in strength or, chiefly in North America, has been entirely replaced. In the U.S.A., where steam locomotive design reached the peaks of power, size and performance only two decades ago, all the Class '1' railroads put together had fewer than 500 steam locomotives left in 1961.

As everyone knows, the victors over steam are diesel and electric traction. The reasons for their conquest are by now common knowledge. Although each diesel and electric locomotive or multiple-unit train costs a great deal more than its steam counterpart, it is much cheaper to operate in the long run. Diesel and electric units have a higher availability for work than steam – that is to say, they can be kept in action without stops for maintenance over much longer periods of time or mileages than a steam engine; the latter's fuel-carrying capacity is of necessity limited, because it needs much more weight of fuel and water to run a mile than a diesel, and it must also be taken out of traffic at least once a day for depot servicing.

Employing diesels or electrics, therefore, a railway can work its trains with fewer traction units than it needed when steam was in command. Moreover, because each locomotive or multiple-unit now needs less time off between jobs to recuperate, and because the superior hill-climbing and accelerative characteristics of diesel and electric traction usually enable their trains to be timed faster, completing their journeys in less time, clever timetabling may make it possible for an engine crew to cover more trips in a shift of work than they could with steam. Thereby the railway extracts more work from its train staff – and derives still more advantage if it can agree with its employees that only one man is needed in the cab of a diesel or electric unit on many journeys; single-manning is quite practicable purely from the driving viewpoint, but some questions of safety and labour politics are also involved. Over the years, the savings I have described will add up to a very convincing total.

In many countries, oil has become a much cheaper locomotive fuel, proportionately to the rail haulage work extracted from it, than coal; thus in Britain the oil consumed by a diesel locomotive costs two-thirds the price of the coal fed into a steam engine on similar work. C.I.E., the Irish railway system, has cut its fuel bill by 45 per cent since it acquired a fleet of diesel locomotives. Good steam coal has become expensive or difficult to mine and the inferior grades are more efficient fuel for electric power stations than in steam locomotives. What is more, the power stations get more work out of the coal; the French railways, thanks to their big post-war electrification programme, have reduced their coal consumption by about 40 per cent over the past ten years.

Coal is dirty to work with. Before the war, when there were not always enough jobs to go round and one with the railway at least promised security, this did not put men off. Today there is full employment in a modern industrial world, with clean working conditions among up-to-date machines, and it is a different story. In the past decade the railways of highly industrialized countries have found it increasingly difficult to attract skilled labour to any task, let alone the upkeep of grimy steam locomotives in gloomy, sooty engine sheds.

Because of the national economic situation at the time, British Railways were not allowed by successive Governments to spend huge sums on new diesel or electric power immediately after the last war. They had to continue building steam – but steam locomotives with a difference from many the L.M.S., L.N.E.R., G.W.R. and S.R. had been turning out. The middle 1930s were memorable for the succession of high-speed lightweight trains. The Great Western set the British pace with its 'Cheltenham Flyer', which in 1932–9 was run at an average of 71·4 m.p.h. over the 77·3 miles from Swindon to Paddington by its 'Castle' class 4–6–0s. In 1935 Sir Nigel Gresley designed for the L.N.E.R. the streamlined 'A4' 4–6–2s to work the 'Silver Jubilee' between King's Cross and Newcastle, 268·3 miles, in four hours; and the first of the type, *Silver Link*, made its début with an electrifying demonstration run in which the 76·4 miles to Peterborough were eaten up in 55 minutes, 25 miles were reeled off at an actual speed of 100 m.p.h. or more, and the top speed reached was 112½ m.p.h. In 1937 the 'Silver Jubilee' was followed by the King's Cross–Edinburgh 'Coronation', taking only six hours for the 393 miles, and the King's Cross–Leeds and Bradford 'West Riding Limited'. In the same year the L.M.S. followed the L.N.E.R. example with its Euston–Glasgow 'Coronation Scot', and for this Sir William Stanier conceived the 'Duchess' Pacifics, which were specially streamlined for the task (this streamlining was removed after the war).

True, the 1930s had seen our railways taking much more interest in general-purpose locomotives, suitable for a wide range of passenger and freight jobs. But concurrently with the multiplication of such outstanding mixed traffic types as the Stanier Class '5' 4–6–0 of the L.M.S., the Gresley Class 'V2' 2–6–2 of the L.N.E.R. and the Collett 'Hall' 4–6–0 of the G.W.R., British engineers were still designing new engines for specific tasks. Right up to the outbreak of war, express passenger locomotive development was particularly absorbing their interest.

On the L.N.E.R., Sir Nigel Gresley was not content with his streamlined, three-cylinder Class 'A4' 4–6–2s, despite 'Mallard's' 126 m.p.h., still unbeaten by steam, in July, 1938, and had his staff at work on designs for an improved 'A4' of higher capacity that could tackle increased loads on the high-speed trains, and for a mighty three-cylinder 4–8–2 which would keep better pace with the streamliners than 4–6–2s on the heavy, everyday East Coast Route expresses. Sir Nigel died during the war, but his successors as C.M.E. continued the L.N.E.R. express passenger Pacific line with the 'A1' and 'A2' classes of three-cylinder 4–6–2 (though the mixed traffic, two-cylinder Class 'B1' 4–6–0 was also born in the post-Gresley period).

For the L.M.S., Sir William Stanier had developed a four-cylinder Pacific type which, in its

Stanier Pacifics of British Railways — (*above*) 'Duchess' No. 46238 *City of Carlisle* climbing Beattock bank with the 'Royal Scot' and (*below*) 'Princess Royal' No. 46210 *Lady Patricia* making for Shap summit with a Glasgow–Birmingham express. [*W. J. V. Anderson*

streamlined guise, had touched 114 m.p.h. on the 'Coronation Scot' demonstration run in 1937, and two years later, in its now familiar, double-chimney, 'disrobed' form, had proved able to lift a 20-coach, 610-ton test train from all but sea level at Carnforth to Shap summit, 31½ miles away and 915ft up, at an average of 56 m.p.h. throughout. From this he was proceeding to a stream-lined 4–6–4, designed to rival an electric locomotive for accelerative ability, when the war frustrated him. Although the G.W.R. had nothing newer to show in the express passenger engine range than its 1927 'King' design when war broke out, it would have produced a Pacific in the post-war period had the idea not been regarded as a luxury in the economic conditions then prevailing.

The most original express passenger locomotives were coming from the S.R., in the shape of O.V.S. Bulleid's unorthodox air-smoothed 'Merchant Navy' 4–6–2s and their 'West Country'

EAST COAST PACIFICS OF BRITISH RAIL-WAYS

Right upper: Gresley Class 'A4' 4–6–2 No. 60026 *Miles Beevor* pulls away from York with a New-castle–King's Cross express.
[*Eric Oldham*

Left: Class 'A1' 4–6–2 No. 60155 *Borderer* approaches Penmanshiel tunnel soon after leaving Edinburgh with the up 'Flying Scotsman'.
[*H. Harman*

Right Lower: Class 'A3' 4–6–2 No. 60061 *Pretty Polly* climbs out of Gran-tham towards Stoke summit with an up Leeds–King's Cross express.
[*C. P. Walker*

and 'Battle of Britain' derivatives. These three-cylinder engines, blessed with one of the most free-steaming boilers ever designed for a British locomotive, were full of innovations, the best-known being their chain-driven valve gear. In recent years, of course, all the 'Merchant Navy' and a good many of the lighter 'West Country' and 'Battle of Britain' 4–6–2s have been rebuilt without their air-smoothed casings and some of their complexities – the chain valve gear, for instance, has been replaced by conventional Walschaerts apparatus – in order to simplify their maintenance at depots, which was perhaps their greatest disadvantage in their original form.

Simplicity was the keynote of the new standard types evolved by British Railways after 1948. To suit the difficult labour and fuel supply conditions of the time, they were to be simple to drive, simple to service at engine sheds and simple to operate – that is to say, they were designed

Most of the Pacific loco-
motives designed by O.V.S.
Bulleid for the Southern
Region of British Railways
have had their original air-
smoothed casing removed
and now look like No.34100
Appledore, seen leaving Victoria station in London for
the Channel coast with the
down 'Golden Arrow' boat
train before the latter's
change to electric locomotive haulage in June, 1961.

[M. Pope

This is the British Railways
standard Class '7', or 'Britannia',
4–6–2 type. No. 70018 *Flying
Dutchman* is speeding past Iver, in
the outer London suburbs, with
a Western Region express from
Paddington to West Wales.

[K. L. Cook

to steam efficiently on the variable quality of coal which was being supplied to the railways, and to have a wide range of use on passenger and goods haulage. Only two of the classes were denominated for specific jobs, a three-cylinder Class '8P' 4–6–2, of which only one example – No. 71000 *Duke of Gloucester* – was built, and the Class '9F' 2–10–0 for freight work; but in practice the ten-coupled engine has proved remarkably versatile and as much at home on a fast merchandise freight or even an express passenger train as on a heavy coal train. Despite driving wheels of only 5ft diameter, as against the 6ft–6ft 8in of engine normally employed on express passenger work, the 2–10–0s have been timed at speeds of up to 90 m.p.h. and those who have driven them maintain that at such speeds they ride as sweetly as Pacifics in good condition; however, they can only be allocated to passenger work in the summer as they are not equipped to steam-heat their trains.

For the rest, the B.R. standard types – the Class '7' and '6' 4–6–2s, Class '5' and '4' 4–6–0s, Class '4', '3' and '2' 2–6–0s, Class '4' 2–6–4 tanks and Class '3' and '2' 2–6–2 tanks – were designed for economical use on all manner of passenger and freight work within their power capacity. Now it is true that a 6ft 8in-wheeled express passenger 4–6–2 is perfectly capable of working a slow and heavy coal train, and on the East Coast Route one sometimes encounters an 'A1' or 'A4' Class Pacific doing just that, but it may have a problem in starting, just as one has in trying to move a motor-car away from rest in top gear, and it will not be working efficiently at the low speeds a B.R. coal train normally maintains. Conversely, a 4ft 6in–5ft-wheeled goods engine is wastefully wearing its reciprocating parts if it is put on passenger work and expected to travel at 60 m.p.h. or more, with its rods and wheels madly rotating. If a steam locomotive is designed for most efficient work on a specific job, it is best to allocate it only to that kind of work, except that adherence to this rule may also be uneconomical; if you have worked a 4–6–2 from King's Cross to Grantham, say, on an express passenger and have no similar train on which it can suitably return home for several hours, but several goods trains, it may be preferable to dispatch it on one of the latter, rather than hold it idle until the right kind of working turns up. On the other hand, you can design a mixed traffic engine which is suited to many different kinds of haulage, and which will greatly simplify the work of those who have to arrange and balance the locomotive workings, out and home, on your railway.

In their Class '7' 4–6–2, the *Britannia*, British Railways' engineers produced one such locomotive. Here is a machine with 6ft 2in driving-wheels which can and has run freely at speeds of up to 90 m.p.h.-plus on the Eastern Region's Liverpool Street–Ipswich–Norwich line passenger trains, but which is also well suited to freight work. In all the standard steam classes the B.R. designers were particularly concerned to provide a high-capacity boiler, but without out-stripping the desirable size and dimensions of the engine, so that there would be a substantial reserve of power for maximum effort. The 'Britannia' Pacific tests on the steeply graded Leeds–Carlisle main line over the Pennine summit of Ais Gill showed that they had succeeded to the extent of creating an engine that, in an emergency, could steam as fast and freely as any of the bigger pre-war express passenger types. With the equivalent of 850 tons behind her tender No. 70005 *John Milton* covered the 22·8 miles from Lazonby to Crosby Garrett, almost entirely uphill and graded at 1 in 100–162 for the last 4 miles, in 29¼ minutes and was not brought below 35 m.p.h. on the steepest part of the climb – though, granted, two firemen were needed to satisfy the boiler's appetite on this occasion. At the other extreme, the boilers and firegrates of the standard locomotives are designed so that no fuel will be wasted when the engines are more lightly loaded. Thus, for example, standard Class '4' 2–6–4 tanks on the Southern Region are not wasting their power when working 3-coach local trains in the Oxted–Tunbridge Wells area during the middle of the day, but have the capacity in reserve to handle some of the business trains between London and this district, which may be three times as heavy, in the morning and evening rush-hours.

Another important feature of the B.R. standard locomotives by comparison with many of their predecessors is their higher 'route availability'– that is, the greater number of lines they can use by comparison with many of their pre-1948 counterparts of similar power. No previous 4–6–2 type has ever had the run of the Great Eastern section of the Eastern Region, but all the G.E. main lines and many of its branches are at the disposal of the 'Britannias', because care was taken to keep the maximum weight on any of their axles down to 20¼ tons, compared with the 22 tons of, say, a Gresley Class 'A3' Pacific, and to restrict their dimensions to achieve clearances

11

that would allow them wide scope on secondary routes. As another example, the S.R. will not allow the L.M.S. Stanier Class '5' 4–6–0 to work over its Mid-Sussex line to Bognor and Littlehampton with summer excursions from North-West London; but it raises no objection to the B.R. standard Class '5' 4–6–0. Thus the standard types are not only available to the compilers of locomotive duties for a multiplicity of jobs, but in many cases over a wider range of routes than their pre-1948 counterparts.

One of steam's major discredits, as already remarked, is the proportion of each day it must spend out of traffic undergoing servicing. After each trip of any length, a steam locomotive must visit a depot for its fire to be raked clear of ash and clinker and, in most cases, for soot to be swept out of the smokebox, where it is apt to collect, blocking the mouths of the lower boiler tubes and impairing steaming. Depending on the capacity of the engine's tender, bunker or tanks, and whether it has been able to pick up water on the move from track troughs during its latest journey, refuelling may well be necessary as well. If a steam engine has finished its day's diagram, the fire will be 'dropped' from the firegrate altogether; when the locomotive has been stabled in the depot and has cooled down, it may be time to scour sooty deposits from the firebox or the inside of the boiler tubes, or to look to the state of the brick arch in the firebox. Then, when the engine is required for duty again, comes the lengthy and time-wasting process of lighting up with a cold boiler; this may take three to five hours from the first firing to the creation of sufficient steam pressure for the engine to be moved when its driving crew sign on for their shift.

At fixed intervals, their length depending on the rate at which each type of locomotive accumulates mileage, a steam engine's boiler must be washed out; with a big express passenger engine it may have to be done every eight or ten days, as against once a month for a small tank engine engaged on local branch work. This immobilizes the engine for several hours. It obviously benefits locomotive utilization if this period of idleness can be exploited to the maximum. For this reason, defects in his engine that are booked by a driver on his repair card, which he must submit to the depot's mechanical foreman before he signs off duty, are deferred, so long as they do not require immediate attention for safety's sake or to make good bad inefficiency, until the engine is taken out of service for a boiler wash-out. On British Railways boiler wash-out time is known as 'X-Day'. In addition to repairs, essential periodical and mileage examinations of the engine's parts are timed to coincide with its 'X-Days'.

Steam motive-power depots built in recent years, such as Thornaby, N.E.R., on Tees-side, which is the most modern on British Railways, have been carefully laid out so that engines coming on shed are serviced on a 'conveyor belt' basis. A disposal track takes them through each item of servicing clear of other shed activity, or allows them to by-pass any stages they do not require if they are merely pausing between 'legs' of a day's work, and the layout is then contrived so that they proceed to their stabling point in the depot without interference with other engines leaving to begin a diagram of work. Wash-out and repair work is carefully segregated from the servicing and preparation of active engines. Further to expedite servicing and return engines to duty as quickly as possible, mechanical devices have replaced some familiar but outdated apparatus; power-operated turntables and mechanically-operated coaling plants, with huge concrete-encased coal bunkers beneath which a locomotive is eased to refill its tender by gravity in a minute or so, are common sights at most large depots, while a few now have gantries spanning a number of shed tracks, and offering to locomotives on each of them a pipe that discharges water or sand at the touch of a button.

The design of the B.R. standard locomotives paid special attention to the simplification of servicing. This was one of the reasons why, except in the unique Class '8' 4–6–2 No. 71000, every one of these types has only two outside cylinders. The *Britannia* was the first British engine of its size and power built without three or four; the third and fourth cylinders would have had to be fitted inside the frames, where they are difficult of access for maintenance. The high running-plates of the standard engines make it easier for maintenance staffs to probe beneath the boiler and between the frames for such work, as they must still do for some parts of the engine's anatomy. Other aids to quick servicing embodied in the B.R. standard types are self-cleaning smokeboxes, rocking grates, self-emptying ashpans and an extended use of mechanical lubricators. In a self-cleaning smokebox (which B.R. denote by a small 'SC' plate on the smokebox door) a

FAMOUS BRITISH RAILWAYS 4–6–0s

Right: Double-chimney 'King' class 4–6–0 No. 6007 *King William III* of British Railways Western Region pulls out of Churston, on Devon's Torquay branch, with an express for London.

[*P. F. Bowles*

Above: A close-up of one of the Western Region double-chimney 'Castle' class 4–6–0s, No. 5073 *Blenheim*, backing on to a London express at Bristol.

[*G. F. Heiron*

Right: A 'Royal Scot' 4–6–0 of British Railways London Midland Region, No. 46146 *The Rifle Brigade*, speeds up the West Coast main line near Hartford, in Cheshire, with an express from the Lake District to London.

[*M. Mensing*

Left: A 'Hall' Class 4–6–0 of British Railways Western Region, No. 6950 *Kingsthorpe Hall*, on express duty, photographed near Cholsey with a London–Worcester express.

[*J. A. Coiley*

Below: A 'Hall' on freight duty – 4984 *Albrighton Hall* approaches Acocks Green, on the Birmingham – Leamington line, with a fully brake-fitted merchandise goods train.

[*M. Mensing*

Below: The British Railways standard Class '5' 4–6–0 type – No. 73138, one of a few fitted with Caprotti poppet valve gear, hurries a Sheffield–London St. Pancras express through Duffield in Derbyshire. [*J. Cupit*

BRITISH MIXED TRAFFIC 4–6–0s

A British Railways lightweight 2–6–0 for mixed traffic work on branch and secondary lines. No. 78044 weighs only 49¼ tons and has a very wide route availability on British Railways.

[R. A. Panting

baffle plate is fixed to create a scouring draught at the base of the smokebox, so that the soot is largely swept away with the exhaust and it is rarely necessary to clear it out more than once a week during servicing. A rocking grate can be agitated from the cab, enabling the fireman to clean his fire of ash and clinker from time to time while his engine is in motion, not solely when it is stationary in a depot yard.

It would not do to leave an impression that the B.R. standard types have superseded the great pre-1948 express passenger designs on the country's major express trains. The 'Big Four' – L.M.S., L.N.E.R., G.W.R. and S.R. – bequeathed to British Railways an ample stock of locomotives specially designed for fast and heavy express haulage, several of which we have already mentioned and which the mixed traffic standard engines were never intended to equal in power or to supplant on their own kind of work. They are yielding only to diesel and electric traction.

A great deal more time and energy has been expended on locomotive testing in Britain since the last war than before it, partly because of the completion at Rugby of the most fully equipped testing plant in the world, and, later, thanks to the provision of mobile test units (see Chapter V). One of the outcomes has been the improvement in detail of several classes, which have ended their careers performing perhaps more efficiently than they did in their youth, bearing in mind the much poorer quality of much of today's coal and the sometimes indifferent maintenance the engines receive, because of staff shortages.

On the East Coast Route, for example, all the Gresley Class 'A3' and 'A4' Pacifics have been equipped with double blastpipes and chimneys, to improve the steaming of their boilers with today's grades of fuel, and have been modified in certain mechanical details to reduce wear and tear of their reciprocating parts and axleboxes. Much of the East Coast main line has already been made fit for speeds of up to 100 m.p.h. in anticipation of dieselization, but it is by no means rare nowadays to find a Gresley Pacific of 1930 vintage getting up to this pace in regular daily service. As to utilization, in 1960–1 a Gresley Class 'A4' Pacific was frequently covering 537 miles in 12 hours, working the 10 a.m. from King's Cross to Newcastle and the 5 p.m. back to London (the latter including a fast 40 minutes start-to-stop timing for the 44·1 miles from Darlington to York) after only 2¼ hours' turnround interval on Tyneside. The double-chimney Gresley Pacifics have been economizing in coal to the tune of about 9 per cent, compared with their previous post-war consumption; moreover, the mechanical improvements have raised

A typical modern tank engine of British Railways for suburban and main line stopping passenger work. It is standard Class 4 2–6–4T No. 80015.

[W. M. J. Jackson

15

Post-war French National Railways express passenger power – the Class '241P' four-cylinder compound 4–8–2, built between 1947 and 1949. Like other high-capacity French steam locomotives, the 35 engines of this class are fitted with mechanical stokers (see page 23).
[*P. F. Winding*

their average mileage between visits to works for general overhaul to about 100,000, a figure which no other Class '8' type in the country can better – and which is about 25 per cent better than the average even in their pre-war prime.

Another major European system which, although it was one of the two principal pre-war pioneers of diesel traction, was showing a keen interest in high-power, high-speed steam locomotives before the last war was the German State Railway. Unlike British railways, the Germans had not been speed-conscious in the first quarter of the century, partly because the German State Railway was not in a position to be ambitious when it was constituted from various state systems soon after World War I. But in the late 1930s there was a sudden upsurge of speed as tracks were refurbished to allow the new German diesel streamliners to make 100 m.p.h.; and steam participated. Some impressive, bulbously streamlined locomotives were designed, including a 4–8–4 and – best known of them – two 4–6–4s with driving wheels as big as 7ft 6in, specifically intended for speeds of over 100 m.p.h. if this were needed to recover lost time. These Class '05' 4–6–4s were required to average 74 m.p.h. throughout their daily run of 178 miles between Berlin and Hamburg and a maximum of 125 m.p.h. was claimed for one of them on a test run.

The last war left the Germans even less in a state to pursue high speed than we were. But like ourselves, they began the peace with ample express passenger and heavy freight power. But they were quick to restore war-damaged or neglected engines to good running order; and since they were soon undertaking both dieselization and electrification, their post-war construction of new steam locomotives has been small. Only 105 were built of the most numerous type, the mixed traffic Class '23' 2–6–2, which calls to mind the B.R. standard outline in many respects, and it was one of these which ended new German steam construction for good in 1960. In 1957 the Germans also turned out the world's last new express passenger design, an extremely interesting Class '10' Pacific of ingenious lightweight design, intended for three-figure speeds. It is equipped with such conveniences as air-operated reversing gear, a device to push the coal from the back to the front of the tender and thereby assist the fireman towards the end of a trip (the ex-L.M.S. 'Duchess' Pacifics and the B.R. Class '8P' No. 71000 also have steam-operated coal-pushers), no fewer than 30 electric inspection lights at various points of the engine and tender, and a well-appointed cab with floor-heating for the crew. Unfortunately, perhaps, the Class '10' was delayed in construction and appeared too late to influence the trend to other forms of traction.

The Germans may not have built much new steam power, but they have been more attentive to improvement of the designs they inherited than British Railways. In particular, many of the Class '01' and '03' express passenger Pacifics have been modified to burn oil instead of coal; the oil is a residual product, which we call 'Bunker C' in this country, left after the refining of such products as petrol diesel and lubricating oil and therefore reasonably cheap – and certainly less expensive than coal. Moreover, the oil capacity of the Pacific's tenders is sufficient for a

British steam power abroad—a Beyer Peacock-built Class '59' 4–8–2 + 2–8–4 Garratt locomotive of the East African Railways

[Blocks courtesy of Locomotive & Allied Manufacturers Association

Above: An English Electric 1,500 h.p. diesel-electric locomotive of the Malayan Railways at Kuala Lumpur

[*Blocks courtesy of English Electric Co.*

Below: An express of C.I.E., the Irish railway system, headed by a Metrovick 1,200 h.p. diesel-electric locomotive. The first vehicle of the train is a four-wheel van carrying a train-heating boiler

[*Blocks courtesy of Locomotive & Allied Manufacturers Association*

greater mileage than the vehicles' coal capacity, so that the engines do not have to be refuelled so often; and, since the firegrate and smokebox do not have to be cleaned of soot or ashes, the engines do not have to spend so long on servicing at their depots. Other devices, such as T.I.A. water treatment to counter agents that scale the boilers (our Bulleid Pacifics of the Southern Region have this French-inspired aid too) and an air-sand boiler tube cleaner that obviates tube-cleaning at the motive depot, have increased the availability of the modernized Pacifics to the point at which they are averaging up to 400–450 miles a day; the regular diagrams for some of them cover as much as 650 miles, more than that arranged for any British steam locomotive – and with bigger loads than in this country, for the German Pacifics are usually in charge of 600-ton trains.

Equally impressive modernization of pre-war steam power was carried out by the French. The French have never minded complicated steam locomotives – for one thing, because of the encouragement their enginemen have always had to take a scientific interest in their charges. A prospective French engine-driver is trained in a locomotive works before he goes on the road (so is a German) and can explain to you every detail of his locomotive's equipment; and a very real inducement to proper management of his engine on the track is the bonus he gets for fuel saving and also, to ensure against any temptation to easy work on that account, one for regaining lost time.

Compounding, never popular in Britain, has been common French practice; this makes extra use of the expansive property of steam by employing it first in high-pressure cylinders, then transferring it, before it is exhausted, to one or two larger, low-pressure cylinders to complete its work of expansion. The possibilities of economy by making the steam do double work are obvious, but it adds considerable complication to maintenance work. Nevertheless, the French saw nothing against the building of some magnificent new compound 4–8–2 and 4–6–4 express engines after the war, and of modernizing some pre-war designs of this type.

Much of this modernization derives from the work of France's greatest locomotive engineer, André Chapelon of the former Paris–Orleans Railway, whose ideas were available to the whole system when the French Railways were nationalized as one concern in 1938. Chapelon's aim was to maintain the heat of steam, and hence its maximum pressure, for as long as possible during

The final development in French National Railways express passenger steam locomotives was this Class 'U' 4–6–4, built in 1949. The four-cylinder compound No. 232.U.1 was photographed entering Paris Nord terminus with an express from Lille, a route from which it is now displaced by 25kV a.c. electrification.

[*P. Ransome-Wallis*

its journey from the boiler through the cylinders to the exhaust. He took an existing Pacific of his railway and set to work. In the inner firebox he inserted thermic siphons, wedge-shaped water containers which are part of the equipment of a B.R. Bulleid Pacific, to increase the heating surfaces at the hottest place and improve water circulation. The boiler pressure and size of superheater were increased; a much larger, smoothly curved steampipe facilitated the passage of steam from regulator to cylinders; and poppet instead of piston valves achieved its smart distribution from the steam chests to the cylinders and then its swift exhaust, the latter being further expedited by the provision of twin blastpipes and a double chimney. The results were outstanding.

The Chapelon principles have been incorporated in many rebuilds of older French types and in several new types. The biggest product of the Chapelon ideas was the Class '242A' 4–8–4 of 1946, a 146-ton three-cylinder compound capable of putting out over 4,000 h.p. On test it has been timed at three-figure speeds and has accelerated a 750-ton train from 17 to 60 m.p.h. up a gradient of 1 in 125 – the equivalent of tackling a load of about 24 British coaches on Shap bank,

One of the Franco-Crosti boilered locomotives of the Italian State Railways. Notice that No. 743.015 has no chimney in the usual place on the smokebox; the exhaust steam is passed through the two bulbous pre-heaters, one on each side of the boiler, and ejected through the two stovepipes, one of which is visible to the rear of the dome.

[P. Ransome-Wallis

between Crewe and Carlisle; on another occasion it reached 70 m.p.h. with the same load from a standing start up a gradient of 1 in 200. Achievements such as this, however, are not defending steam against the growing spread of the French electrification network, with the great savings in consumption of coal that have been achieved through feeding it to power stations instead of into locomotive fireboxes.

Over the years many locomotive engineers have produced devices to improve the low thermal efficiency of the steam engine, which has always been one of the biggest discredits to set against its simplicity and robustness; that is to say, the engineers have tried to get more work for each unit of fuel burned. One of the most recent of these inventions originated in Italy and has made curious shapes of many Italian locomotives. An idea of this kind is of particular interest to the Italians, who have built new steam locomotives since 1920, but whose railways have not had the

18

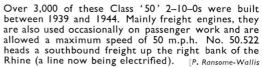

GERMAN FEDERAL
STEAM LOCOMOTIVES

Over 3,000 of these Class '50' 2–10–0s were built between 1939 and 1944. Mainly freight engines, they are also used occasionally on passenger work and are allowed a maximum speed of 50 m.p.h. No. 50.522 heads a southbound freight up the right bank of the Rhine (a line now being electrified). [*P. Ransome-Wallis*

Post-war German Federal designs – (*above left*) 4–6–2 No. 10.002, the last word in express passenger locomotives of which only two were built in 1956; and (*above right*) one of the standard mixed traffic 2–6–2s of Class '23'.

[*P. Ransome-Wallis, L. Marshall*

Since the war the Germans have modernised the impressive Class '01.10' 4–6–2s built in 1939 with massive new boilers and oil-firing equipment; here No. 01.1082 heads the southbound 'Adria Express', bound from Copenhagen to Italy and Yugoslavia.

[*P. Ransome-Wallis*

money to press on fast with the electrification which abundant sources of natural water power make the obvious choice for rail traction throughout most of the country. Thus a considerable amount of steam working persists – with expensive, imported coal. The device is the Franco-Crosti boiler and its derivatives.

We have seen the Crosti version of the boiler on ten British Railways Class '9' 2–10–0s, Nos. 92020–9. In the Crosti boiler the heat gases generated in the firebox pass through the boiler tubes in the normal way, but in the smokebox they are diverted into the tubes of one or more pre-heaters; the Crosti boilers on the B.R. 2–10–0s had one pre-heater, slung below the boiler, but the Italian engines have two, one on each side. In the pre-heater the gases raise the temperature of the boiler feed-water and are then exhausted through a chimney – or chimneys – ahead of the cab; if the engine has a chimney in the usual place, on the smokebox, its only function is to create a draught when the engine is raising steam before duty (as on the B.R. 2–10–0s), but the

A post-war design for R.E.N.F.E., the 5ft 6in gauge Spanish National Railways system. This 145-ton oil-burning 4–8–4 of Class 242.2000 was turned out in 1956.

Italian Crosti engines have oddly naked smokeboxes devoid of any conventional chimney. The aim of the Franco-Crosti or Crosti boiler is both to obtain more work from fuel consumed and to reduce boiler maintenance costs by nullifying some of the harmful effects of water admitted at low temperature to a fully steaming boiler.

In practice, the results have been rather mixed. The long and tortuous path the gases have to follow before they are exhausted impairs the draught, affecting the steaming and also making the Crosti engines rather dirty to work, because the draught is not strong enough to blast the exhaust clear of the cab. The weaker velocity of the heat gases also allows the sulphur in coal to react more readily with the products of combustion and form sulphuric acid, with serious corrosive results. The outcome in this country has been the modification of the 10 Crosti 2–10–0s as orthodox steam locomotives, although they still retain their curiously high-pitched boiler, with the now redundant pre-heater below it. Other countries in which Franco-Crosti engines can be seen besides Italy are Germany, where several 2–10–0s have been fitted, and Spain, which has one.

Talking of the B.R. 2–10–0s, No. 92250 of this class has been modified with another device

NARROW GAUGE GIANTS

Beyer-Garratt articulated locomotives on the metre gauge East African Railways — (above) a close-up of the leading unit of a '60' Class 4–8–2+2–8–4 fitted with a Giesl oblong exhaust ejector; and (right) one of the bigger '59' 4–8–2+ 2–8–4s, built in 1955, heading a freight train in the area of Mombasa.

[East African Railways & Harbours

STEAM BEHIND THE IRON CURTAIN

A 135-ton Class 'IS' 2–8–4 of the Soviet Railways, built in 1936 heads an express from Odessa to Moscow. The appearance of the locomotive reflects Soviet interest in U.S. railroad methods at the time it was built.

[J. N. Westwood

The pride of the Soviet Railways steam locomotive fleet are the Class 'P36' 4–8–4s built in 1950. They are responsible for many of the principal passenger services including those from Moscow to Leningrad and Brest Litovsk; a pair of them are seen leaving the main station in Leningrad.

[J. N. Westwood

A modern three-cylinder 4–8–4 tank of the Czechoslovak State Railways, built by the Skoda works in 1956. These locomotives are used on a variety of haulage, from expresses in heavily graded territory to local passenger trains and short distance heavy freights.

[A. E. Durrant

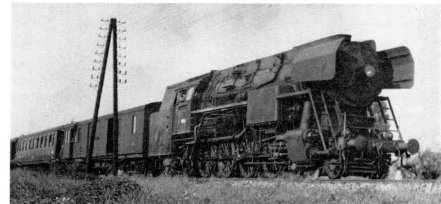

A handsome Czech two-cylinder 4–8–2 of Class 475 makes an all-out uphill effort with freight near Bratislava.

[A. E. Durrant

intended to improve thermal efficiency – and one that seems likely to be rated more successful than the Franco-Crosti boiler by future railway historians. This is the Giesl Oblong Ejector, which originated on the Austrian Federal Railways and to whose locomotives, in particular, it has been extensively applied. In latter-day steam locomotives the increasing size of boilers has left little room above them for a chimney of sufficient length to serve efficiently its purpose of creating an adequate blast for draughting the fire; to offset this deficiency, engineers have resorted to reduction in the area of the blastpipe caps at the base of the smokebox which, combined with growing cylinder dimensions, has tended to create high back pressures and negative work in the cylinders when a modern engine is being worked hard. Dr. Giesl's invention aims to overcome this problem with what is basically seven blastpipes in line, all exhausting into a common chimney of narrow oblong shape and great depth inside the smokebox, and one which tapers steadily from its base to its rim. It is claimed that the Giesl Ejector, because it reduces back pressure by minimizing the shock loss incurred during the mixing in the smokebox of exhaust steam from the cylinders and the gases drawn through the boiler tubes from the firegate, increases the cylinder power at any given steaming rate, thereby cutting coal consumption.

MECHANICAL STOKERS

A mechanical stoker facilitates the firing of steam locomotives with poor quality, small-sized coal; it also enables firing to be maintained at an intensive rate that would exhaust a human fireman, in conditions where steam locomotives are required to put out high power continuously. On British Railways only three locomotives – Class '9' 2–10–0s Nos. 92165–7 – have mechanical stokers. The illustrations show (*right*) the cab of a South African Railways Class 'GMAM' Beyer-Garratt, with the stoker engine, steam-powered from the main boiler, conspicuous on the left

of the footplate; and (*below*) a diagram of a typical mechanical stoker, showing the worm which conveys the coal from the bunker on the left to the distributing table on the far right, from which jets under the fireman's control spray the fuel evenly over the fire grate. The fireman can control the firing rate by adjustment of the stoker engine's speed.

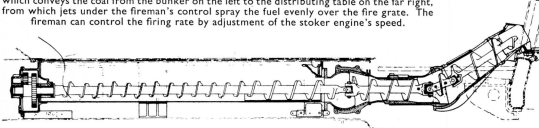

A memory of the heyday of U.S. steam might – three Class 'EM-1' 2–8–8–4s of the Baltimore & Ohio Railroad, all three engines with their tenders totalling 1,236 tons, battle upgrade in Ohio with a 9,000-ton haul of coal in 121 bogie hoppers. Although built as recently as 1944–5, giants like this have been ousted by diesel traction all over the U.S.A.

[J. William Vigrass]

Super power of the 3ft 6in gauge – the Class '25' 4–8–4 of the South African Railways, built in 1953. The massive 12-wheel tender houses apparatus to condense the locomotive's exhaust steam back to water to re-fuel the boiler. The provision of water supplies has always been a problem in some areas of the S.A.R. system and these condensing engines can operate for up to 700 miles at a stretch without refilling their tender tanks.

Apart from Austria and Britain, railways in Czechoslovakia, Spain, New South Wales, Germany, India, East Africa and Poland have tried the Giesl Ejector and the results they report largely substantiate its inventor's claims. The East African Railways, for example, which have fitted 4-8-4 + 4-8-4 Beyer-Garratts (a type discussed below) with them, affirm that, with the locomotives really extended, 15 per cent more power has been produced, while a Giesl-equipped Class 'C36' 4-6-0 of the New South Wales Government Railway has shown a coal saving of 8 per cent over its standard sisters on comparable work. The Austrians, too, are highly satisfied with their many Giesl Ejector locomotives.

The Austrians, however, have set a term on steam working and have already electrified a third of their route mileage. The Dutch and the Swiss have virtually eliminated steam. In fact, the only thing that retards the demise of steam in Western Europe is shortage of money or technical resources in some of the poorer countries, such as Greece, Portugal and Spain – or, to go a little farther afield, Turkey.

The Spanish and Portuguese railways are unique in Western Europe for their 5ft 6in gauge, compared with the 4ft 8½in that is standard elsewhere, and this has allowed the Spanish to design some of the most massive locomotives to be seen this side of the Iron Curtain. As recently as 1956, R.E.N.F.E., the Spanish national railway system, was adding a completely new locomotive class to its stock – a bulky, 145-ton, oil-burning 4-8-4 with many modern refinements, designed to head expresses over the steeply graded but not yet electrified sections of the main line between Madrid and Irun. Knowing that they would have to persist with steam power in numerous areas of their system for many years to come, the Spanish limited their new construction under a 1949 standardization scheme to five big modern types, ranging from 2-10-2 freight engines to the outsize 4-8-4s I have just mentioned. Whereas the British Railways standard locomotive plan included small engines for the lighter duties, the Spanish have carried out no post-war replacements of that kind; thus R.E.N.F.E. is now a railway of picturesque contrasts, with long chimneyed, squat-boilered veterans of a hundred years' or more service on the more menial haulage tasks working side by side with ultra-modern main-line machines unsurpassed for size and elegance on the European continent. Although of recent years there has been a considerable improvement as a result of electrification and the introduction of some diesel traction, Spanish train services generally are well below the average European standard of speed, largely owing to the difficult country the routes have to traverse; thus the 1956-built 4-8-4s of Class 242.2000 are designed with 6ft 3in driving-wheels for sustained speeds no higher than 60 to 70 m.p.h., which is generally the maximum permitted with steam traction in Spain.

Behind the Iron Curtain at least one state, Czechoslovakia, although it has since the last war turned out some fine new steam designs with the most up-to-date equipment, has ended steam building. The Russians, like British Railways, decided to make an end of steam in 1955, by which time post-war Soviet industry in the establishment of new hydro-electric power stations and the development of internal oil supplies had made the switch practical politics. But whereas in Britain the change was to be gradual and some construction of new steam power continued, the Russians put a stop to steam locomotive building almost overnight. Under the Soviet régime, passenger traffic had never been regarded by the Russian railways with the same interest as freight and the great majority of latter-day Russian steam power consists of burly goods engines that in many cases look like refugees from the U.S.A. – and not surprisingly so, since from 1930 onwards the Russians tried to model their 5ft-gauge railway system on the American pattern of high-capacity motive power and long trains. As a result, most Russian passenger trains which are still steam-worked, except on the trunk routes, are handled by the Class Su 2-6-2, basically a design originated in 1910, but one which was still being built as late as 1951 and which finally totalled some 3,750 engines.

In the 1950s, however, the Russians did begin to demonstrate more interest in passenger traffic and the very last new Soviet steam locomotive design to proliferate in any number was the handsome, streamlined Class P36 4-8-4, a 135-ton machine with 6ft 0¾in driving-wheels, of which some 250 were put into service between 1954 and 1956. Visitors to the Soviet Union report that the Russians are extremely proud of these locomotives, which are vividly painted light green with bright red wheels and lining; they keep them as far as possible on the routes frequented by tourists, such as the main line from the Polish frontier to Moscow and the Moscow-

Leningrad service, which the Russians recently graced with their first mile-a-minute expresses. At the time of writing, steam power is still entrusted with about two-thirds of Russian traffic, but the Soviet authorities hope – optimistically, many observers consider – to have reduced this proportion to about 20 per cent by 1965 and to have eliminated steam traction altogether by 1970.

There are a few under-developed areas of the world – parts of South America and Africa – where the cheapness of local labour, the need to restrict the technical complexities of the equipment they use and in some cases the cheapness of fuel, have encouraged, and still do, perseverance with steam. In a way, some of these railways have operated the most remarkable steam locomotives of all, especially those of the African continent. Most of the principal systems were laid to narrow 3ft 6in or metre (3ft 3⅜in) gauge, because of the difficulty of the terrain and the need to save money in construction; the sharper curves possible with the narrow gauge, compared with the standard 4ft 8½in gauge, enable a railway to go round obstacles such as hills or gullies that otherwise would have to be cut through, tunnelled through or bridged at high cost. Yet numerous African systems have employed bigger locomotives than any seen in this country.

On some African routes the gradients are so severe and the curves so sharp that if conventional tender engines within loading gauge limits and of an axle-load suitable for the track were used, there would either have to be excessive employment of assistant locomotives or else train-loads would have to be reduced uneconomically. The invention of a Victorian locomotive engineer named Garratt and its development by the British firm of Beyer Peacock solved the problem. The Garratt gives you virtually two locomotives for the axle-loading of one. It does so by providing two sets of driving-wheels and cylinders, to spread the weight of one locomotive as it were, and each set of wheels is made to carry a share of the fuel supplies; between these two units there is slung on strong frames a massive boiler, which can be of a much larger diameter than on a conventionally arranged locomotive because it is not mounted above any inside reciprocating parts.

In modern times a system like the metre gauge East African Railways, whose route between Mombasa and Nairobi climbs 5,600ft with a ruling gradient of 1 in 60 and a sharpest curve of 350ft radius, and beyond Nairobi to a 9,136ft-high summit, has worked most of its traffic with Beyer-Garratts. Its last, the '59' class, the biggest machines ever built for the metre gauge, are 4–8–2 + 2–8–4s with a 7ft 6in diameter boiler, weighing 252 tons, touching 13ft 5½in at maximum height above the rails and stretching over 104ft in length. By comparison, a British Class '9' 2–10–0's boiler is only 6ft 1in in maximum diameter; it weighs 142 tons with tender and is only 13ft 1in from rail to chimney-top and a mere 66ft 2in over buffers from the front of the engine to the rear of the tender. Yet the heaviest weight on any of the Beyer-Garratt's axles is only 21 tons. These '59' Class engines can happily tackle 1,200-ton loads on the 1 in 60 grades of the Mombasa–Nairobi line. The 214-ton Class 'GL' 4–8–2 + 2–8–4 Beyer-Garratts of the 3ft 6in-gauge South African Railways, which are the most powerful steam locomotives ever built outside the U.S.A., have a maximum axle-load of only 18½ tons, which is two tons below that of a B.R. 'Britannia' Pacific.

In Africa, however, even the Beyer-Garratts are yielding. Despite local sources of coal, the South Africans are seeking diesel locomotives and the East Africans took delivery of their first main-line diesels from English Electric in 1960. What has been described as the most human machine man ever devised, the steam locomotive, is slowly but steadily passing into history the world over.

26

DIESEL TRACTION AND GAS TURBINE LOCOMOTIVES

ON the morning of April 18, 1934, a sleek, stainless steel 4-car streamliner glided out of Denver, in the western American state of Colorado, and set out eastwards on a run that turned one of the most important pages in railway history. Named the *Pioneer Zephyr*, the train was bound for Chicago, 1,015 miles away. That evening it rolled dramatically into the heart of an exhibition that was being held in the 'Windy City', having covered the whole 1,015 miles without an intermediate stop at an average of 77·6 m.p.h. all the way. In the *Pioneer Zephyr*, the diesel engine – and the General Motors engine in this unit was itself a pioneer specially suitable for rail traction purposes, unlike those in previous rail diesel vehicles – first showed practically what it could offer the world's railways in the way of sustained high speed and continuous action without pause for servicing.

The U.S. public was craving for speed; and several railroads hastened to satisfy them with trains on the *Pioneer Zephyr* pattern. But, while the public was happy, the railroads could see the *Zephyr's* limitations. It was an indivisible, articulated unit – that is to say, each of its four coaches shared a bogie with its neighbour; if the power plant was defective, the whole train was out of action – the coaches could not be separated and coupled to another locomotive. The next step was a separate main-line diesel locomotive (diesel shunters and independent railcars had been operated in the U.S.A. for some years previously).

By 1937 the standard streamlined U.S. diesel passenger locomotive began to take its grip of the American railroads, showing the way to the future with such achievements as the 2,227-mile haul of the Santa Fe 'Super Chief' from Chicago to Los Angeles without any engine change *en route* and at an average throughout of over 50 m.p.h., including stops. We were also becoming accustomed to the American multiple-unit locomotive. These 1,800-h.p. machines were produced with or without cabs, to demonstrate another advantage of diesel traction – the practicability of driving two or more locomotives coupled together from one position, by the coupling of electro-pneumatic control circuits between them. The cableless units, or 'boosters' as the Americans call them, were less expensive to build than those with cabs and control desks and they saved the cost of extra crews to drive them. Moreover, they could be added to a cab unit only when operating requirements demanded additional power, whereas one very high-powered locomotive would have to carry always a high-capacity, more-expensive-to-maintain engine that would be fully employed only for a proportion of its daily work.

The use of booster units was increased when the Americans turned their hand to the production of a main-line diesel freight locomotive in the late 1930s. Across the Atlantic a freight locomotive means a machine that may have to move trains a mile or more long and 5,000 tons or more in weight, and which may have to lift its trains in some parts of that vast country over summits higher above the sea than any mountain in the British Isles. The prototype freight locomotive designed by the Electro-Motive Division of General Motors in 1939 was therefore a 5,400-h.p. type, but with the total power output coming from four 1,350-h.p. units – two with cabs at each end and two cableless in the centre; this quartet was designed to be split in two and operated as two 2,700-h.p. twin-unit locomotives as desired. The starting tractive effort of the four-unit locomotive was about twice that of the largest steam locomotive operated by any U.S. railroad at the time. In the next year the prototype was demonstrated successively on 20 major U.S. railroads, proving time and time again that it could outdo steam in sheer weight haulage and in performance upgrade – and, what is more, at a saving in fuel costs. Almost at once, 13 of the railroads who had entertained the diesel visitor placed orders for their own freight diesels.

Above: Why U.S. railroads are turning to high horsepower diesel 'hood' units – a sextet of older General Motors 1,500 h.p. freight locomotives, some with cabs, some cabless and including one 'hood' unit, is needed to maintain the $20\frac{1}{2}$ hr schedule of this crack New York Central merchandise freight over the 960 miles from Chicago to New York. [*H. H. Harwood Jr.*

Below: Diesel railcars, U.S. style – two stainless steel Budd 'R.D.C.'-type cars of the Jersey Central lines. [*W. A. Burke Jr.*

Above: Close-up of a typical General Motors diesel-electric express passenger triple-unit totalling 4,500 h.p., with a 'booster' between two cab units; this one belongs to the Santa Fe Railway. [*Santa Fe Railway*

AMERICAN DIESEL TRACTION

Below: The modern trend in U.S. diesel power, to expedite heavy freight haulage, is to locomotives like this trio of General Motors 'SD–24' 2,400 h.p. units heading a Union Pacific freight through mountainous terrain. [*Union Pacific*

Above: This typical U.S. 1,000-h.p. diesel 'switcher', or shunter, was photographed in the docks area of New Orleans. [*B. A. Butt*

Wartime conditions highlighted the diesel locomotive's advantages of almost constant availability for work, because it needs so little time out for servicing, and probably helped to accelerate its take-over of the U.S. railroads. From 1943 new steam locomotive construction tailed off sharply to nil by the end of 1950; by then industry was hard put to satisfy the pace at which U.S. railroads, with few exceptions, wanted to replace their steam power (encouraged by very useful hire-purchase agreements with the manufacturers, let it be added). Now even the most recent and massive products of the U.S. steam locomotive builder's art, such as the Union Pacific 540-ton 'Big Boy' 4-8-8-4s built in 1941-4, the biggest in the world, and the Norfolk & Western 2-6-6-4s, which have reached 60 m.p.h. with 6,500-ton trains, have been retired; dieselization of the whole U.S. railroad scene is over 90 per cent complete. While British Railways are only in the early stages of their dieselization, many U.S. diesel locomotives have seen over 20 years' service and need replacement or remodelling; and with the attainment of this phase in U.S. dieselization there is a noticeable change in the type of diesel locomotive employed – but of that more anon.

Dieselization of the Canadian Pacific and Canadian National Railways did not begin on any scale until 1950, but has proceeded with such pace that by 1961 both systems had completely abolished steam working. The locomotives are of the standard U.S. General Motors, ALCO or Fairbanks-Morse firms' pattern, but built by Canadian companies under licence. These Candian diesel-electric locomotives afford an excellent example of the diesel's availability for continuous running on the transcontinental trains of the two systems, which are their most successful passenger operations – for, in Canada, as in the neighbouring U.S.A., the railways are fighting a losing battle on this front. Two 1,800-h.p. diesels work unchanged for $70\frac{3}{4}$ hours throughout the 2,881 miles between Montreal and Vancouver with the Canadian Pacific's luxury 'Canadian', a recently built train of sleek, stainless steel stock with palatial day and night accommodation, including 'Vista-Domes', of the kind sported by the U.S. transcontinental express described in Chapter IV. A third diesel unit is attached to help the train up the long ascents which are as steep as 1 in 50 or worse for 22 miles on end to a summit 5,339 ft. above the sea in the rugged Rocky Mountains, where 'Canadian' passengers revel in some of the most majestic scenery any railway journey in the world can offer.

Now we must trace the pre-war developments in the territory of the other chief diesel traction pioneer, Germany. The Germans drew world attention to their advance in diesel traction for express passenger purposes earlier than the Americans, for it was in 1933 that they first astonished us with the 'Flying Hamburger', a 77-ton 2-car articulated streamliner driven by a pair of Maybach 410 h.p. engines. Timed from Berlin to Hamburg, 178 miles, at $77\frac{1}{2}$ m.p.h. from start to stop, the 'Flying Hamburger' was the first regularly operated train in world railway history that simply had to run some parts of its journey at 100 m.p.h. if it was to keep schedule, seeing that severe speed restrictions were in force at certain points *en route* and these had to be offset elsewhere. The streamliner's success was instantaneous and by the outbreak of war in 1939, German diesel streamliners were criss-crossing their country over routes specially relaid and re-aligned for 100 m.p.h. travel, offering German businessmen a network of services by which they could leave cities like Munich, Nuremberg, Stuttgart, Frankfurt, Cologne and Bremen in the morning, reach Berlin with ample time for a day's business and be back home by nightfall. The fastest of the streamliners, the 'Flying Cologner', daily ran the 158 miles from Berlin to Hanover at an average of 83 m.p.h. and the $109\frac{3}{4}$ miles from Hanover to Hamm at 82 m.p.h. in the course of a day's round trip of 719 miles. So popular were these services that by 1939 the streamliners had become 3-car units and in some cases two of these were needed on one train to cope with the patronage. Unlike the Americans, the Germans did not produce any significant diesel locomotives until after the war, which put paid temporarily to diesel development in Europe.

After their earliest 'Flying Hamburger' units, the Germans parted company with American practice in one very important particular, presenting other railways that have followed the dieselization path with an agonizing choice between the two pioneering leads. The matter on which the pioneers differ is the method of transmission of power from diesel engine to road wheels. A steam locomotive generates its propelling force – steam – outside its cylinders, by external combustion, and can therefore transmit full power to the pistons at the moment of starting.

WHEEL ARRANGEMENT	NOTATION
○ INDIVIDUALLY DRIVEN AXLES	○○ COUPLED WHEELS	◉ CARRYING WHEELS
	B
	Bo
	Bo-Bo
	Bo+Bo
	B-B
	C
	Co
	C-C
	Co-Co
	Co+Co
	A1A-A1A
	1Co-Co1
	1-Co-Co-1
	2-Co-Co-2
	1-Do-1
	2-Do-2
	1A-Do-A1

WHEEL ARRANGEMENTS

The basis of the system used to describe diesel (and electric) locomotive wheel arrangements is that the non-motored, carrying axles are indicated numerically, but that the number of driving axles is shown by letters. Thus, a four-wheel carrying bogie is denoted as '2'; in the driving wheel group, 'A' signifies one motored axle and 'B', two motored axles, etc. Each group of wheels is separated by a dash, except in the case of driving bogies that are not entirely independent of each other, but linked by an articulated joint, or whose axles are connected by cardan shafts to a common engine, when a 'plus' sign is substituted. When the suffix letter 'o' is added to a driving axle group, it indicates that each axle has its own motor.

The diesel engine is an internal combustion machine; it developes its power by the ignition of a carefully controlled mixture of air and oil inside its cylinders. It must therefore be able to turn over, free of any connection with the locomotive's road wheels, in order to develop its tractive effort: and, when that has been done, a transmission is required which can absorb the power from the now active engine and pass it smoothly, without a snatch, to road wheels which at first are inactive.

The simplest and cheapest type of transmission is mechanical, by which the engine output is transmitted through a fluid flywheel, or fluid coupling, and a multi-speed gearbox to a final drive linked directly with the road wheels. In general, a mechanical transmission is suitable only for low-powered traction units of not more than 450 h.p., because higher loads and faster speeds inflict uneconomic wear and tear on the gearbox. Its use is thus confined to shunting locomotives with diesel engines of comparatively low r.p.m., or to diesel railcars employing bus-type diesel engines of high r.p.m. but low power. Thus on British Railways it is found on the majority of diesel multiple-units, but in the locomotive fleet only on shunters of 200 h.p. or less.

Until the 1950s most countries followed the American example by selecting an electric transmission for medium and high-powered locomotives. In this system the diesel engine powers a generator producing current for conventional electric traction motors, mounted on the bogies of the locomotive, which drive the road wheels through suitable gearing. The Germans' first 'Flying Hamburger' units were diesel-electric, but soon they were employing hydraulic transmissions. In the early stages of hydraulic transmission development it was little more reliable for employment in high-powered traction units than a mechanical transmission, but technological progress after the war was rapid and the Germans have evolved hydraulic transmissions that are perfectly efficient with engine outputs of up to 2,000 h.p.

The fundamental part of a hydraulic transmission is a torque converter. Its function is to multiply the torque, or power, of the diesel engine in the same way as the gearbox of a mechanical transmission; but, since the link between the engine and the road wheels in the torque converter is fluid and not frictional, it can transmit smoothly a much higher power. The three basic parts of a torque converter are: the impeller, which is a centrifugal pump; the turbine wheel, which is the driven member: and the fixed guide, or reaction, wheel. The impeller is mounted on the drive shaft from the engine. When the latter rotates, the impeller forces the fluid filling the torque converter casing on to the turbine wheel of the driven shaft to the road wheels. The turbine wheel is induced to rotate in sympathy and from its blades the fluid passes to the first ring of guide vanes on the fixed guide wheel, which redirect it to a second set of turbine blades, thereby imparting more torque to the turbine wheel, and hence to the driven shaft to the road wheels. This sequence may be further repeated, depending on the design of the torque converter and the amount of torque multiplication desirable to the performance of the loco- motive. A very useful characteristic of the hydraulic transmission is that it transmits maximum power when the output from engine to impeller is greatest and the turbine wheel of the torque converter is stationary – that is, in a transmission system employing only one torque converter, when the road wheels are stationary; thus a hydraulic transmission produces a particularly good starting tractive effort. In a modern high-power diesel-hydraulic locomotive there is usually a se- quence of two or more torque converters, as in the Voith system, or a single torque converter is linked with an automatically operated multi-speed gearbox, as in the Maybach Mekydro system, so that a fresh power transmission peak is available in successive speed ranges – starting, medium and high speed, for example; each torque converter or gear is automatically brought into opera- tion as the road and diesel engine speeds enter the range for which it is designed.

The advantages of electric transmission centre mainly on simplicity. The main components, the generator and traction motors, are orthodox, self-contained machines that are easily installed or removed for maintenance. By contrast, a hydraulic transmission, including cardan shaft drives to the road wheels, is complex and more troublesome to maintain – when it needs mainte- nance, that is; the Germans contend that it requires relatively little, and claim that cardan shaft drives will function for about 200,000 miles without need of inspection. The cardan shaft drives from the torque converter to the powered axles of a diesel-hydraulic locomotive's bogie, however, act as a coupling which helps to give it something like a 30 per cent advantage in starting adhesion over a diesel-electric unit of comparable power. Another advantage claimed for the hydraulic transmission is that it has no moving and stationary parts in contact and that its main components are immersed in oil and encased to the exclusion of dirt or moisture, which can make mischief in a force-ventilated electric transmission. But the most important point made by hydraulic transmission proponents is that their system is considerably less bulky than the rival and saves tons of locomotive weight, which means either an economy in fuel or that a heavier load can be hauled, since the locomotive has less of its own tonnage to move. Moreover, if the locomotive is less bulky, it is safe to rest all its weight on the driving wheels and adhesion is thereby enhanced; there is no need to distribute some of the tonnage over idle carrying wheels. In the high power ranges, the multi-stage torque converter transmissions employed make a diesel-hydraulic locomotive more expensive to buy than a diesel-electric of comparable power. For this reason, many more railways are using diesel-hydraulic shunters than there are operating high-power main line units with this kind of transmission.

The Germans supported their claims with the major diesel traction event of 1961. So much have the Germans advanced with their hydraulic transmissions that even the Americans, wedded for years to their own manufacturers and their diesel-electric products, have been mightily impressed. In the case of two railroads operating in the mountainous west of the U.S.A., the Southern Pacific and the Denver & Rio Grande Western, the interest was keen enough to order 4,000- h.p. diesel-hydraulic locomotives from the German firm of Krauss Maffei. Each of the two systems is now taking delivery of three of these machines, which are the first imported main- line diesel locomotives to run on any U.S. railroad. Whereas the latest U.S.-built 2,400-h.p. freight diesel-electric on two six-wheel bogies weighs 146 tons, the German 4,000-h.p. diesel- hydraulic, which incorporates two Maybach Type MD-870 engines, each with its own three- torque converter transmission, is mounted on two six-wheel bogies, and weighs only $128\frac{1}{2}$ tons – yet it can produce 66 per cent more power than the U.S. diesel-electric. As a result, the Rio Grande is planning to use its three German imports as a multiple-unit on freight haulage in a heavily graded territory where previously eight home-built 1,500-h.p. diesel-electrics were needed to pull and push each train. Assuming that the German machines prove as reliable as their less powerful and highly developed relatives have done in the very different railway con- ditions of their own country, the reduction in the number of locomotives required by the two U.S. railroads will mean a big saving in maintenance and crew costs; moreover, the better than 50 per cent economy in locomotive weight for horsepower output should mean that the trains can either be run faster or that the loads carried can be increased.

[*Continued on page* 35]

DIESEL ENGINES IN BRITISH USE

This cutaway drawing shows clearly the triangular arrangement of the Napier 'Deltic' engine used in the 3,300-h.p. Type '5' diesel-electric locomotives of British Railways.

KEY

1. 'BC' crankshaft
2. 'BC' crankcase
3. Inlet piston
4. Exhaust piston
5. Crankcase breather
6. 'AB' crankcase
7. 'AB' crankshaft
8. Main bearing cap
9. Crankcase tie-bolt
10. Drain oil manifold
11. Air inlet gallery
12. 'A' camshaft casing
13. Fuel injection pump
14. Exhaust manifold
15. Water pump
16. Water pump and pressure oil pump drive gear
17. 'CA' crankshaft
18. Cylinder block tie-bolts
19. Cylinder liner
20. 'C' cylinder block
21. Blower flexible drive shafts

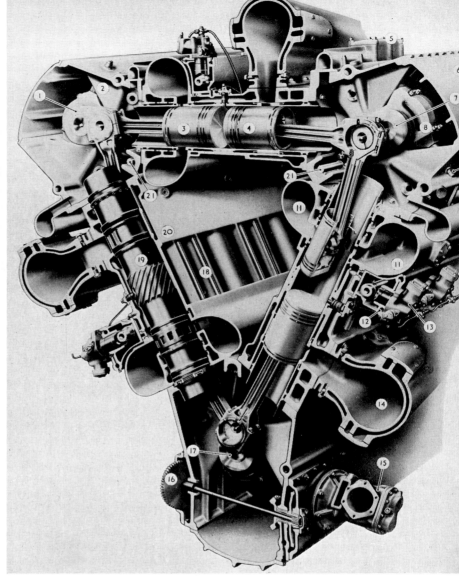

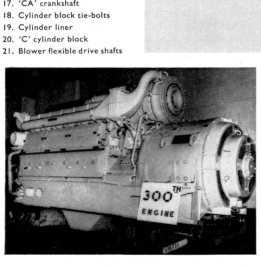

These pictures give some idea of the greater degree of compactness possible in a high-speed diesel engine arrangement. On the left is the medium speed 750 r.p.m. Sulzer Type 12LDA28–B diesel engine of 2,500 h.p. employed in the Type '4' diesel-electric locomotives built in B.R. workshops. On the right is the high-speed 1,500 r.p.m. Maybach Type MD870 engine, rated at 1,900 h.p. in the German Federal Railway Type 'V160' diesel-hydraulic locomotive.

The diesel-powered de luxe express of the Trans-Australian Railway between Port Pirie and Kalgoorlie, a distance of 1,108 miles. This run includes 328 miles across the Nullarbor Plain, featuring the longest stretch of straight line in the world. The journey takes 25½ hours. The diesel locomotive is of U.S. pattern built in Australia under licence

[Blocks courtesy of J. Stone & Co. (Deptford) Ltd

A Metropolitan-Vickers (A.E.I.) 3,820 h.p. electric locomotive on the Sydney–Lithgow line of the New South Wales Government Railways

[Blocks courtesy of Locomotive & Allied Manufacturers Association

THE DIESEL ENGINE

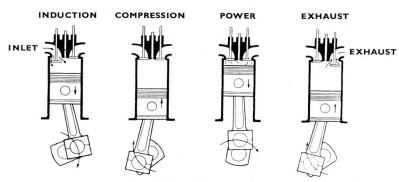

THE FOUR-STROKE CYCLE

THE name 'diesel' commemorates the man who developed the principle on which a diesel engine works (Dr. Rudolf Diesel, who produced the first working example in 1895.) The other name for a diesel engine – 'compression ignition engine' – points the difference between a petrol engine and an engine of the diesel type. In the former, the piston is moved by the ignition, through an electrical spark, of petrol induced into the cylinder; the ignition causes an explosion and a rapid expansion that thrusts the piston down the cylinder. In the diesel engine there are no sparking plugs. The ignition is produced when the piston, on its upward stroke, compresses and heats air, while fuel oil is injected into the cylinder just before maximum compression is reached; the mixture explodes of its own accord to impart movement to the piston.

Two methods of arranging this process of admission of air and fuel and then the compression and ignition are used in modern locomotive diesel engines. They are the two-stroke cycle and the more generally favoured four-stroke cycle; the former has the piston making one power stroke for every revolution of the crankshaft, the latter one power stroke for every other revolution of the crankshaft.

The sequence of events in a cylinder working on the four-stroke cycle begins with the opening of inlet valves in the cylinder head through which the piston, descending the cylinder, sucks in air; this is known as the induction stroke. Then follows the compression stroke; the air inlet valves are closed and the piston rises, compressing the air and raising it to a high temperature. As the piston reaches the end of this stroke, oil is injected into the compressed air in a fine spray and instant ignition occurs, starting the downward power stroke of the piston. Finally there is the exhaust stroke; the piston rises up the cylinder once more, expelling the burnt gases through exhaust valves which open at the beginning and close at the end of the exhaust stroke. Then a new four-stroke cycle begins with the induction stroke.

In a cylinder operating on the two-stroke cycle, the intake and exhaust strokes of the four-stroke engine are covered by a separate pump. As the piston is thrust down the cylinder by ignition, it uncovers ports in the wall of the cylinder, through which air is forced by a blower. The air scours, or 'scavenges', the cylinder of the burnt gases from the previous ignition, discharging them through exhaust ports that open as the piston reaches the end of its stroke. As the piston returns up the cylinder, the exhaust ports close and the air admitted through the inlet ports is compressed by the rising piston to 500 lb. per sq. in. or more. At the top of the stroke oil fuel is injected in the form of a fine spray, which mixes with the compressed air, now raised in temperature to over 1,500° F., and is at once ignited. The violent combustion forces the piston downward, thus initiating another power stroke.

Theoretically, it will be seen, the two-stroke cycle should make for a more powerful and efficient engine, since power is produced for every rotation of the crankshaft; moreover, this has the advantage that variations in cylinder temperature are kept to the minimum. These advantages are offset by the fact that the 'scavenging' methods of the two-stroke are not as efficient as those of the four-stroke cycle, so that a two-stroke is by no means twice as powerful as a four-stroke.

A two-stroke arrangement which should be mentioned, as it is employed in the British Railways 'Deltic' locomotives, is the opposed piston type, in which two pistons face each other in the same cylinder. The pistons move towards each other, compressing the air between them, and fuel is injected through the wall of the cylinder at the point where they are about to meet; ignition thrusts both pistons away from each other. As one piston nears the end of its stroke it uncovers exhaust ports, through which the burnt gases escape; a split-second thereafter the other piston uncovers induction ports in the walls at its end of the cylinder, through which a blower forces air into the space between the pistons. Then another compression stroke begins.

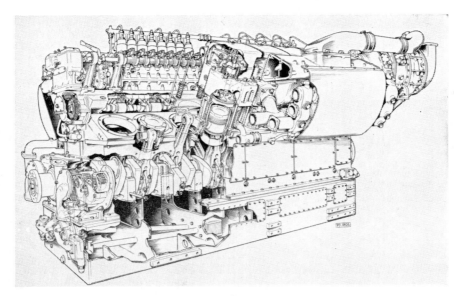

Cut-away drawing of the Davey Paxman 16-cylinder YHXL 'V'-type diesel engine fitted in the British Thomson-Houston Type I diesel-electric of British Railways.

'Pressure-charging' can increase the power output considerably and is widely employed on diesel locomotives. This involves the provision of a compressor, driven by the engine shaft on some smaller engines, but usually by an exhaust gas-powered turbine (a 'turbocharger') or electrically (on some diesel-electric locomotives) to compress air to high pressure before it is induced into the cylinder. If pressure-charged air is used, a greater weight of fuel can be injected into the cylinder, for the increased amount of oxygen in the air will ensure its efficient combustion; the result is, of course, much higher power – as much as 50 per cent in the case of four-stroke engines. Power can be increased still further by 'inter-cooling', a device which uses the engine-cooling water to cool the pressure-charge and further to increase its density.

The arrangement of the cylinders in a diesel engine depends on the number, and the number depends on the power required. Engines of three, four, five, six or eight cylinders can have the cylinders arranged in line, either vertically or horizontally (for underfloor mounting on a railcar), the pistons being connected to a crankshaft at the base of the cylinder bank.

The most common 'multi-bank' arrangement is probably the 'V'-form engine, with the cylinders in two equal banks angled like a 'V' from a crankshaft at the base. Another alternative is to arrange them in parallel vertical banks, with the main engine shaft between and beneath them, gear-driven from the crankshaft of each cylinder. Some more complicated arrangements have been devised for opposed-piston engines, such as the 'Deltic' (see page 32). In a multi-cylinder engine the order in which the cylinders fire is carefully arranged to exert the most even turning movement on the main crankshaft.

The most vital part of a diesel engine is the fuel injection system, for it is this which controls the speed of the engine. First, if gravity feed is not employed, a feed pump is needed to lift the fuel from the storage tank, but it is the injection pump, to which the fuel is delivered, that is the nerve-centre of the system. Each cylinder of the engine has its own injector pump, either as a separate assembly or as an element of a complete pump unit for the whole engine, and it is here that the flow of fuel is controlled, Moreover, to atomize the fuel within the time of about $\frac{1}{300}$ sec., the injector pump must create a pressure of anything up to 10,000 lb./sq. in. before the needle valve of the injector will open and allow the fuel to spray from the injector nozzle into the cylinder to mix with the compressed air. To ensure efficient injection the most meticulous construction and maintenance of the pump and the injector is required, and working to such fine limits as $\frac{1}{20,000}$ in. may be necessary. Equally vital is scrupulous cleanliness of the oil and the working parts of the oil system, the air supply, and the filters which maintain this condition, for the slightest degree of dirt can seriously affect engine performance.

The driver is not always allowed complete control over the supply of fuel to the engine, because there may be some engine speeds at which damaging vibration is set up. It is not uncommon, therefore, to find the controller marked off in four or five set speeds, or notches, which avoid the critical rates that cause trouble. Naturally, these controller notches take no account of the load behind the locomotive, so a governor is necessary to adjust the fuel supply automatically up or down, according to the load.

DIESEL TRACTION AND GAS TURBINE LOCOMOTIVES

[*Continued from page* 31]

In this comparison the difference is not only in transmissions, but in the type of engine employed. The weight-saving in the German locomotives has been achieved at the cost of daring in engine design as well as the employment of hydraulic transmissions. Very little in this world is obtained for nothing; and that is true of any increase in horsepower per ton of diesel locomotive weight or cubic foot of its size. It is not every railway system outside Germany which is convinced that the complications incurred in their alliance of high-speed engines with hydraulic transmissions involve no sacrifice of all-important reliability.

Increasing the r.p.m., or working speed of a diesel engine is one way of boosting its power without having to enlarge its size; but it stands to reason that, the faster moving a piece of machinery is, the quicker will wear show, the higher therefore may be the maintenance costs and the stronger may be doubts as to its reliability in service. In a diesel shunter, which is not called upon for great feats of performance, but which must be essentially an utterly reliable unit that ought not to have to go near a depot throughout a week's work, a low-speed engine is customary. The standard 6-coupled diesel-electric shunters of British Railways, for example, chiefly have engines of English Electric or Blackstone manufacture in the 350–400-h.p., 630–750-r.p.m. range of ratings. These are without doubt the greatest successes among our diesel locomotives so far, showing immense savings over the steam locomotives they have replaced; whereas the latter always burned fuel in lulls between work as well as on the shunting job, and needed daily servicing, the diesels can be sent out with enough fuel in their tanks for several days' activity, during which they require little or no attention, and can be shut down completely when they are not actually engaged on marshalling.

In general, British Railways have also opted for bulky low-speed engines, or engines just within the medium speed range of 800–1,200 r.p.m., for their main-line locomotives, preferring to bet on reliability against the weight-saving economies of high-speed engines that they do not regard as fully proved. The first Type '4' diesel-electric locomotives in the 2,000–3,000-h.p. range, of which most have so far been ordered, for example, have a Sulzer 2,500-h.p., 750-r.p.m. engine (Nos. D1–193, under construction at Derby and Crewe works) and an English Electric 2,000-h.p., 850-r.p.m. engine (Nos. D200–399, an English Electric design manufactured at Newton-le-Willows and Darlington). The employment of engines of this character is a principal factor in the locomotives' respective weights of 138 and 133 tons, which has to be spread over eight axles, of which six are powered. By contrast, the 2,200-h.p. Type '4' diesel-hydraulic type built by Swindon works and the North British Locomotive Co. for the Western Region of British Railways (No. D800–70), which is derived from the German Federal Railway's 'V200' type, employs ingenious methods of lightweight construction and is powered by two 1,100-h.p., 1,500-r.p.m. high speed engines of German devising that are built in Britain under licence; it weighs a mere 78 tons and needs only four axles, all powered, to distribute its weight to the satisfaction of B.R. track engineers.

Two more British designs demonstrate that engine design is a vital factor in the achievement of more horsepower per ton of locomotive weight, whatever the transmission. In the autumn of 1961 the Brush Group produces its prototype *Falcon* locomotive, which is a diesel-electric but has an output of 2,800 h.p. for only 108 tons' weight, so that it can be carried on two 3-axle bogies without exceeding a maximum axle-loading of 18 tons. A major difference between the Brush *Falcon* and the other two B.R. Type '4' diesel-electric designs mentioned in the previous paragraph is that the *Falcon* uses two Maybach high-speed engines of 1,400 h.p. apiece, of the same German family as those in the Swindon-built diesel-hydraulic Type '4s' – or 'Warships', as they are commonly known, because they have been named after British naval vessels.

The other British Railways main-line diesel-electric design with one of the best power-to-weight ratios in the world is the English Electric 3,300-h.p. 'Deltic', of which 22 (Nos. D9001–22) are now coming into service to revolutionize the operation of East Coast Route express passenger traffic. It produces its 3,300 h.p. for a total weight of only 106 tons and is the most powerful diesel-electric single unit in the world (though it is beaten by the six 4,000-h.p. diesel-hydraulics built by Krauss Maffei for the U.S.A., which we have mentioned, and by a 4,000-h.p. locomotive employing the same power plant which the Henschel firm is now building for its home

[*Continued on page* 39]

Top right: Western Region 2,200 h.p. diesel - hydraulic 'Warship' class locomotive No. D805 *Benbow* approaches Newton Abbot with a Sunday Paddington – Plymouth express. This is the British Railways Type '4' version, with two high-speed Maybach engines, of the German 'V200' type illustrated on page 44.

[*D. S. Fish*

A British Railways Type '1' diesel-electric locomotive for light mixed-traffic work – the B.T.H. 800 h.p. version with Davey Paxman engines: No. D8208 was photographed at Liverpool Street station in London on a late evening parcels train.

[*M. Mensing*

Right centre upper: Diesel-electric traction on the Southern Region of British Railways – 1,550 h.p. Type '3' No. D6538, built by the Birmingham R.C. & W. Co., and 1,160 h.p. Type '2' No. D5003, built in B.R. workshops, but both with Sulzer engines, work multiple-unit through Canterbury East with the Victoria–Dover 'Golden Arrow' boat train.

[*S. C. Nash*

DIESEL LOCOMOTIVES OF BRITISH RAILWAYS

Below: A 170 h.p. diesel-hydraulic 0–4–0 shunter standing alongside one of the former Lancashire & Yorkshire Railway steam 0–4–0 saddletanks, built in the 1890s, which it has replaced in the Liverpool area.

[*British Railways*

Right centre lower: The new look in Great Northern line London suburban traffic – 1,365 h.p. Brush Type '2' diesel-electrics Nos. D5608 and D5604 head past New Barnet with city-goers' trains from Cambridge and Hatfield to London's Broad Street terminus.

[*J. F. Aylard*

Bottom right: One of the production series of 3,300-h.p. English Electric 'Deltic' Type '5' diesel-electric locomotives at speed between Darlington and York during a test trip from Edinburgh to King's Cross. The first coach in the train is a dynamometer car recording the locomotive's performance.

[*E. Sanderson*

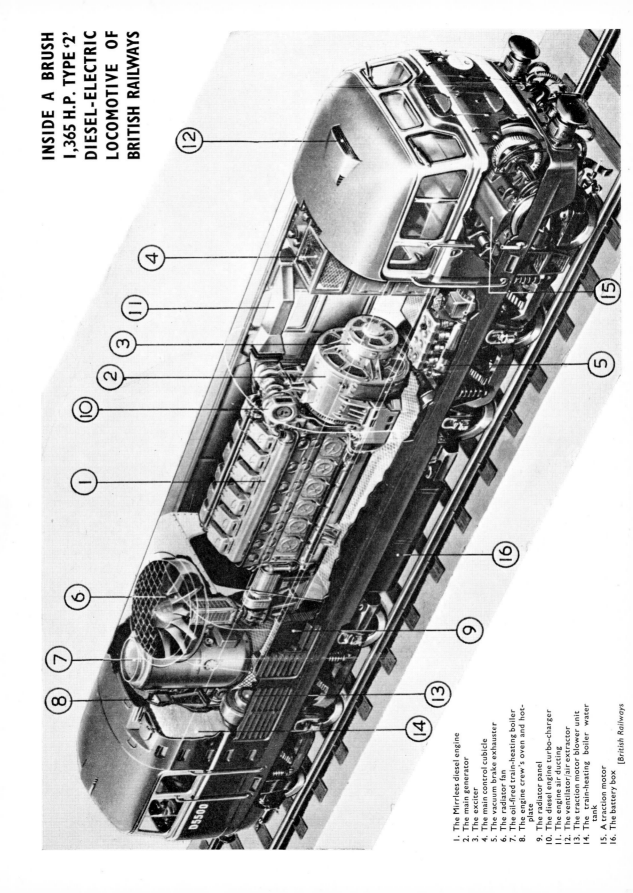

INSIDE A BRUSH 1,365 H.P. TYPE '2' DIESEL-ELECTRIC LOCOMOTIVE OF BRITISH RAILWAYS

1. The Mirrlees diesel engine
2. The main generator
3. The exciter
4. The main control cubicle
5. The vacuum brake exhauster
6. The radiator fan
7. The oil-fired train-heating boiler
8. The engine crew's oven and hot-plate
9. The radiator panel
10. The diesel engine turbo-charger
11. The engine air ducting
12. The ventilator/air extractor
13. The traction motor blower unit
14. The train-heating boiler water tank
15. A traction motor
16. The battery box

[British Railways]

[*Continued from page* 35]

German Federal Railway). The kernel of the 'Deltic's' high power within such restricted body space is the adoption of the opposed piston principle for an ingeniously compact triangular cylinder arrangement (*see page* 32) in its two 1,650-h.p. Napier 'Deltic' engines, from which the locomotive takes its name.

The most numerous users of high-speed engines on British Railways are the multiple-unit diesel railcars that have transformed local and cross-country workings throughout the country. The engines in this case, however, are comparatively low-powered ones of 150 to 238 h.p., derived from the type of diesel engine used for years past in heavy road vehicles. The number – and power – of engines per railcar set varies according to the character of the service for which the vehicles are built. Most of the powered cars have two British United Traction (Leyland or A.E.C.) 150-h.p. six-cylinder engines, each driving one of the car's bogies through a mechanical transmission; in a 2-car unit, one or both cars may be powered according to need, in a 3-car unit two cars are powered, and in a 4-car unit with these engines, two cars are powered. Some sets employ two Rolls-Royce 180 h.p. engines on each powered car, and there are some 2-car units on the L.M.R. of which each car is powered by a single Rolls-Royce 238-h.p. engine.

In the early years of British Railways' experience with these diesel multiple-units it became obvious that the 150-h.p.-engined cars were under-powered for the toughest assignments on which it was intended to replace steam with a greatly improved service. Latterly, therefore, we have seen a trend to engines of higher capacity in the railcars. The 4-car sets which have been constructed at Derby works for the Marylebone–Aylesbury and St. Pancras–Bedford suburban services in the London area each have two power cars equipped with two Rolls-Royce 238-h.p. engines – and, incidentally, with hydraulic transmission, which has been adopted for several Rolls-Royce engine applications to these railcars. The highest powered of any diesel multiple-units so far built for British Railways (with the exception of a rather special case, the luxury Pullman units discussed in Chapter IV) are the 6-car 'Inter-City' diesel-mechanical sets for the Hull–Leeds–Manchester–Liverpool 'Trans-Pennine' service, which have stiff gradients such as the 7-mile climb at 1 in 96–105 westward out of Huddersfield to negotiate in their Pennine journey via Standedge Tunnel; no fewer than four of their six cars each mount two B.U.T. 230-h.p. engines.

The arguments on the relative reliability of high- and medium- or low-speed diesel engines crop up even among the B.R. diesel railcars, for the Southern Region, because of its experience with electric traction and the possibilities of standardizing electrical components, decided on electric instead of mechanical transmissions for the multiple-units it operates in Hampshire and between London and Hastings, and soon will do in South Devon and on the Oxted line; and for duty with electric transmission it settled on a 600-h.p., 850-r.p.m. English Electric engine. Because of its bulk, this engine (which is fitted in the ratio of one power car to a 3-car unit) has to be mounted above the frames of the vehicle, taking up space available for passengers or luggage in a diesel-mechanical car whose compact, horizontal high-speed engine can be slung underneath the body; moreover, an S.R. diesel-electric power car weighs 56 tons, compared with the 35½ tons of the heaviest diesel-mechanical power car elsewhere on B.R. But to offset their disadvantages and their higher first cost, the Southern's diesel-electric units have required less maintenance and have shown a higher availability for work than the diesel-mechanical units on other Regions; on the average, each 3-car unit on the Hampshire services covers 365 miles a day – roughly the equal of a daily run from London to York and back, calling at every intermediate station – and one Sunday duty covers over 500 miles, with the unit inactive at terminals for no more than 1½ hours of the 16½ hours it is in service, shuttling to and fro mainly between Southampton and Alton.

Such high daily mileages as this are possible because diesel multiple-units can carry enough fuel for 350–400 miles' travelling and need no servicing after a routine inspection before the day's work begins. It is only once in five days (seven days, in the case of the S.R. diesel-electric units) that they need to be taken out of traffic for more extended maintenance work. At terminals the train is reversed simply by the driver walking from the cab at one end to the cab at the other, saving more time.

The possibilities of the multiple-unit principle with regard to locomotives have already been

Above: For high-density suburban traffic – four-car diesel-hydraulic units on the Bedford service, each equipped with four 238 h.p. Rolls-Royce engines, at London's St. Pancras terminus.

[*M. Mensing*

BRITISH RAILWAYS
DIESEL MULTIPLE-UNITS

Above: The typically attractive interior of a B.R. suburban diesel multiple-unit, showing the view ahead through the driving cab; this is a unit built by Park Royal. *Left:* For inter-city service – the buffet and a first class saloon of a six-car set on the 'Trans-Pennine' service between Hull, Leeds, Manchester and Liverpool.

[*British Railways*

Right: One of the six-car 'Trans-Pennine' units, powered by eight 230 h.p. B.U.T. engines with mechanical transmissions, passes through Manchester Victoria. *en route* from Liverpool to Hull.

[*I. G. Holt*

discussed; they are wider still with these railcar sets. There is fascinating study in the working arrangements of a diesel depot like Leeds Neville Hill or Darlington, whose duties are cleverly dovetailed in some instances, so that single units, which have been operating separately on diverse branches during the day, meet conveniently, say, at York, to augment a peak evening train to Leeds or Darlington on which extra accommodation is desirable; that job done, the units are separated and disperse to further branch duty. Each unit added to a train brings with it a proportional addition of diesel engine horsepower to match its weight, so that there is no problem of overloaded power plant when train capacity is increased; and the electro-pneumatic multiple-unit controls are simple to connect by means of universal 'jumpers', which group numerous cables in a single plug, after which one driver can manipulate all the units in his train from the leading cab.

The neat driving desk of a British Railways diesel-mechanical multiple-unit. On the extreme left of the desk is the throttle and in the centre the gear-change lever, with the vacuum brake handle to the right of it.

What does the higher availability for work of a diesel traction unit, by comparison with steam, mean in terms of economy in power? It means, for example, that the Great Eastern Line of the Eastern Region will by 1962 have replaced the 660 odd steam locomotives that it needed for all its main-line passenger and freight services before modernization began with a mere 250 main-line diesel locomotives, concentrated on four depots – Stratford, Ipswich, March and Norwich. The diesel locomotives are sent out from these depots on five-day 'cyclic' diagrams, or duties; they are given a routine daily inspection while 'on tour', but it is only each sixth day that they are booked for a lengthy visit to their base depot for maintenance

Dieselization, again, means that the Western Region will need fewer locomotives for its Paddington–Penzance main-line workings. It can work its Type '4' diesel-hydraulics throughout without change, partly because of their greater endurance, partly because their reasonable axle-loading, despite their power, allows them over the Cornish main line beyond Plymouth, from which the ex-G.W. 'King' 4–6–0s were barred; previously Paddington to Plymouth was the limit of locomotive working.

As a final example, the 22 'Deltics' of the East Coast Route, distributed between the Eastern, North Eastern and Scottish Regions, should be adequate to replace 57 steam Pacifics; each of the 3,300 h.p. diesels is expected to average over 200,000 miles a year, compared with the 75,000–100,000 miles put up by steam 4–6–2s on this route. On test the prototype 'Deltic' has run the 29·1 miles from Peterborough to Grantham, which includes the 15-mile Stoke bank (1 in 178 at its steepest), in 25 minutes with a 550-ton load, and in the reverse direction I was in the train when it accelerated a 360-ton load from 25 to 105 m.p.h. within eight miles. Ability of this kind has enabled the King's Cross–Newcastle–Edinburgh timetable to be accelerated to the shortest basic times ever (but with considerable additions to allow for slowings for increasing modernization work on the track and stations) in 1962, as described in Chapter V, so that by running faster than steam, each locomotive covers more mileage per day. London–Edinburgh–London or *vice versa* – 787 miles – is a standard day's work for a 'Deltic', whereas London–Newcastle–London – 567 miles – has been thought an arduous day's diagram for steam power.

Discussing diesel-electric locomotives earlier, I referred to simplicity of component installation and maintenance. To a greater or lesser degree this applies to all diesel units and permits economical repair by replacement. If a diesel engine or the transmission of a locomotive or multiple-unit is defective it need not mean that the whole vehicle is immobilized; the faulty item can be removed and repaired at leisure, so to speak, while the vehicle itself is sent back in traffic with a replacement assembly. Practice of this kind is greatly facilitated by rigorous standardization of design.

A large measure of the success of dieselization in the U.S.A. can be credited to emphasis on standardization from the earliest days. The small number of major manufacturers has concentrated on production of the minimum of basic locomotive types, with as many standard components as possible, which they have then offered to U.S. railroads with or without optional extras to suit individual customers' needs, such as steam train-heating boilers or dynamic braking (a useful device on locomotives likely to do heavy haulage on routes with long, steep gradients; it reduces wear and tear on train brakes by reversing the diesel-electric locomotive's traction

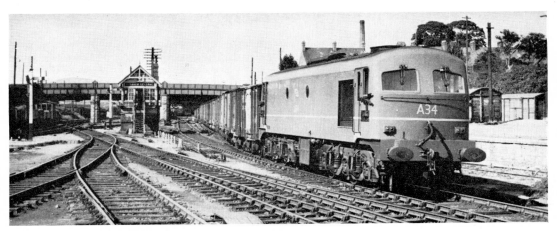

Dieselization of C.I.E., the national railway system of Eire, is almost complete. Built by Metropolitan-Vickers with Crossley engines, 1,200 h.p. diesel-electric No. A34 leaves Dundalk with a freight for Dublin.

[*F. Church*

motors so that they are opposed to the momentum of the train as generators, which dissipate the energy as heat through vents in the locomotive's roof). These extras do not vary the essential design of the locomotive.

Today two huge firms command all but the whole of the U.S. diesel locomotive market – ALCO and General Motors – with only two other firms, Fairbanks Morse and the General Electric Corp. making any sort of competitive showing, but far, far behind the 'Big Two'. As a further example of the standardization in the U.S.A., even today the latest locomotives from the Electro-Motive Division (E.M.D., as it is familiarly known) of General Motors are equipped with a development of the two-stroke '567' series engine first introduced by this firm in 1938; over the years it has been uprated in power by modifications and increased degrees of pressure-charging, and it is now available in five versions ranging from an 800-h.p. six-cylinder to a 2,400-h.p. sixteen-cylinder – but the basic design is the same. Again, although E.M.D. may still build an occasional streamlined cab unit of the 1940–50 outline to its old designs (and is also busy revamping its first generation of U.S. diesels with new engines and later refinements, now that they are already reaching the end of their first life), its new sales of main-line locomotives to U.S. railroads are virtually all of three mixed traffic types.

Several European railways have adopted lightweight four-wheel railbuses to reduce the running costs of rural branch lines. With varying economic success, British Railways have also experimented with these vehicles; this is an A.C. Cars-built 11-ton diesel railbus, serving the Western Region's Cirencester branch from Kemble, where it is seen connecting with a main line express.
[P. J. Sharpe

In the last few years there has been a domestic American trend away from the streamlined cab unit. U.S. rail passenger business has slumped in face of the severest road and air competition anywhere in the world, as we shall see later in this book, and there is much less enthusiasm for sleekly-styled, exclusively passenger power. Most railroads are buying general purpose 'hood units' – the U.S. term for locomotives which house their power plant in utilitarian bonnets with detachable side panels that simplify maintenance. Current E.M.D. main-line sales are almost exclusively of two 1,750 h.p. 'hood unit' designs, one on four- and one on six-wheel bogies, and of a 2,400-h.p. type on six-wheel bogies; the latter is one of the new high-powered machines finding great favour in the U.S.A., as the railroads seek to move heavy freight tonnage more economically by raising speeds and reducing maintenance costs through a reduction of the number of units worked in multiple. The variations to meet the traffic needs of individual railroads that are possible with one standard diesel locomotive design are shown by the fact that the General Motors 2,400-h.p. machine is available arranged for speeds of up to 90 m.p.h., or for a lower maximum but a greater tractive effort – i.e., intended chiefly for heavy freight haulage – mainly by altering only the gear ratios of its traction motors. This is another advantage of dieselization, without sacrifice of standardization.

The other dieselization pioneer, Germany, pursues standardization just as keenly. The German Federal Railway's 2,400-h.p. 'V200' (the uprating of this type to 2,700 h.p. is contemplated) and 1,200-h.p. 'V100' locomotives, its three- and four-car 'VT08' and 'VT13' high-speed multiple-units, and its luxury 'Trans-Europe Express' trains, all of them diesel-hydraulic, employ identical diesel engines and transmissions. Not only that, but the engines are types by three different

A French Railways lightweight diesel railcar and trailer leave Bourges; notice the cockpit driving cab on the power car, a design feature which the French favoured on some of their early diesel railcars.
[C. G. Pearson

GERMAN DIESEL TRACTION

Below: Two of West Germany's standard diesel locomotive classes – the 1,200 h.p. type 'V100' for secondary routes (*upper*); and the 650 h.p. type 'V65' for shunting and local trip work (*lower*). Both are diesel-hydraulic.

Above: One of the German Federal Railway's four-car Type 'VT08' diesel-hydraulic units for express passenger work. This one was photographed on the 'Hans Sachs' service between Dortmund and Nuremberg at Wurzburg.

[*P. Ransome-Wallis*

Below: This was the kind of diesel multiple-unit with which, in the 'Flying Hamburger' and other services, the Germans led the European rail speed race before World War II. It was photographed after the war at Vienna on the run to Prague and East Berlin.

[*A. Hofbauer*

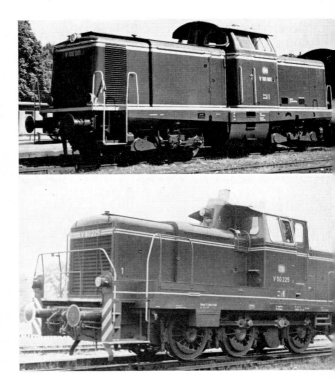

Right: Western Germany's standard express passenger diesel is the 2,400 h.p. type 'V200' diesel-hydraulic, on which the Swindon-built 'Warship' of British Railways is based.

[*D. G. Clow*

manufacturers – M.A.N., Maybach and Daimler-Benz – and the transmissions are Voith and Mekydro; each type of engine and each kind of transmission is freely inter-changeable. For the future the German Federal Railway has decided that all its traffic requirements can be met by only five standard diesel-hydraulic locomotive types (apart from shunters): a 650-h.p. Type 'V65' 0–6–0 for local work, a 1,200-h.p. Type 'V100' B-B for secondary routes, a 1,900-h.p. Type 'V160' B-B for mixed traffic, a 2,400-h.p. 'V200' B-B for express passenger work and possibly the projected 4,000 Type 'V320' C-C, of which a prototype is now building, for the heaviest expresses and special high-speed trains.

The ability to prove a design, both of a locomotive and of its major components, in lengthy service in the home country has been of enormous help to the Americans and Germans in capturing world markets for what are usually adaptations of their standard domestic products to suit overseas operating conditions. Concealed or overt subsidies from their Governments in one form or another have also been worth a great deal, let it be added.

Of European countries, Belgium, Denmark, Norway and Spain are operating diesel loco-

One of the three-car diesel-mechanical multiple-units built by Fiat for Spanish National Railways express work. The centre car includes a kitchen and bar.

motives either exported intact from the U.S.A. or built on this side of the Atlantic to U.S. patterns and with U.S. technical assistance. The Spanish National Railways' 1,600-h.p. diesel-electric units built by ALCO could be taken for the property of any U.S. railroad, so typically American is their streamlined nose, although they are un-American in that the opposite, box-fronted end of each unit also features a driving cab; their U.S. counterparts, of course, are so rarely employed as single units that they do not need to be double-ended for driving purposes.

The Danish and Norwegian diesel locomotives are mainly Swedish-built units of 1,900–1,950 h.p. with electric transmission, built by Swedish firms to a U.S. pattern and with General Motors engines (both countries also employ diesel railcars and have some electrified mileage). About three-quarters of Danish train mileage is now achieved with diesel traction – but a notable proportion of it is made, strange as it may sound, over water. Denmark consists of a number of large islands, as well as the big promontory of Jutland which thrusts northward towards Norway and Sweden. As the country's capital, Copenhagen, stands on the most easterly of the islands, Zealand, the operation of the Danish State Railways presents some problems. The

10,535ft Storstrom Bridge, the longest in Europe, links Zealand by rail with Falster island in the south and the 3,865ft Little Belt Bridge carries the country's principal main line, from the west-coast port of Esbjerg to Copenhagen, out of Jutland to the neighbouring island of Funen. But a 16-mile-wide channel, the Great Belt, divides Funen from Zealand; and over this waterway, as over others that intersect import Danish rail routes, trains that include important traffic between Germany and Scandinavia have to travel by large, three-track ferries that make four or five trips each way a day.

Norway was a disconcerting country for its original railway-builders. Over 1,100 miles long, it is in places no more than 20 miles wide; at least half of it is some 2,000ft or more above sea level, while fjords bite deep into the western coastline. Its most striking main line links the nation's two principal cities, the North Sea port of Bergen and the capital of Oslo. The route lies across the Hardanger Mountains, a range

A main line diesel locomotive of the Soviet Railways. This is one half of the twin-unit 'TE–7' type, which has a total output of 4,000 h.p. and a maximum speed of 87½ m.p.h.

4,000ft or more in height, and since in these northern latitudes the snowline never rises above 3,000ft or so, the Bergen–Oslo line, which reaches a 4,293ft summit near Finse, had to be built and still is operated for part of its length in snow, winter and summer alike. Miles of avalanche shelters and snow fences protect the railway from the elements and during the winter four rotary snowploughs are almost continuously at work. This trunk route is now almost completely dieselized with the locomotives previously mentioned and diesel-hydraulic luxury multiple-units, employing German Maybach engines and Mekydro transmission.

Even in a British Commonwealth country like Australia, the U.S. locomotive industry has a foothold through firms that have been established in that country to manufacture American-type diesels. The country's biggest operator of diesel traction, the New South Wales Government Railways, uses main-line locomotives built in its own country by the firms of Goodwin and Clyde, but these are respectively associates of ALCO and General Motors. Of the other State railway systems, Victoria has given its allegiance so far to Clyde-G.M. and South Australia to Goodwin-Alco; only Queensland, having evaluated some prototypes from different manufacturers before buying in bulk, has opted for British design in its latest purchases of 1,650-h.p. diesel-electric locomotives built by the Australian subsidiary of English Electric. Some of the Australian State railways have lately invested in diesel-hydraulic shunters and there are hints that electric transmission has not conclusively won the day for Australian main-line locomotives.

The first Australian system completely to dieselize its operations was the Commonwealth Railways, which were set up by the Federal Government to establish land communications in the wild 'outback' of the country where no other organization was anxious to risk its money in railway-building. The principal artery of the Commonwealth Railways is the famous 1,108-mile trans-Australian line across the desert between Port Pirie, South Australia and Kalgoorlie, Western Australia, which is dead straight for 328 consecutive miles of its passage of the treeless Nullarbor Plain. The Commonwealth Railways have some Sulzer-engined, Birmingham Railway Carriage & Wagon Co.-built locomotives on other parts of their system, but this vital national link is now dominated by Clyde-G.M. 1,500–1,750-h.p. diesel-electric locomotives (hauling, incidentally, luxury air-conditioned trains with day and night accommodation that

American diesel export – a 1,900-h.p. diesel-electric built to the American pattern in Sweden, with the General Motors '567' series 16-cylinder engine, for the Norwegian State Railways. It is seen at Finse, 4,000 ft up in the Hardanger mountains between Bergen and Oslo.
[*G. W. Morrison*

were built in Western Germany or Japan – the Commonwealth is certainly not an assured market for British railway products these days!). For many years the trans-Australian and other Commonwealth Railways lines were run at a loss, but since the inception of diesel traction a profit has been earned on operations; no small factor in this change is the fact that, when steam ruled the trans-Australian line, about 25 per cent of the traffic comprised fuel and water to feed

British diesel export – two 1,800 h.p. 'hood' units built by English Electric at work in the Kikuyu country of Kenya on the East African Railways. On the steep Mombasa–Nairobi line a steam Garratt of Class 59, which entered service in 1955, can haul 1,200 tons. Working in multiple, two of these new Class '90' diesel locomotives, with a lighter, 12.8-ton maximum axleload, are able to tackle a 1,400-ton train.
[*East African Railways and Harbours*

the locomotives in the unpopulated wastes of the desert, whereas the diesels are much more independent of intermediate stops to take on fresh supplies.

The rapidly modernizing Australian railways have a great deal to display that is impressive, including very intensive electric suburban operations with up-to-date multiple-units in their big cities such as Sydney and Melbourne (where the 16-platform Flinders Street station handles some 2,000 trains a day), but they are hampered by one major drawback to integrated operation in competition with rival forms of transport – differing gauges. South Australia and Victoria built to 5ft 3in gauge, Western Australia and most of Queensland to 3ft 6in, and New South Wales and the Trans-Australian to 4ft 8½in. Changes of train for passenger and freight traffic are therefore inevitable in a journey across the country. At long last, after years of agitation, action is being taken to unify on the standard 4ft 8½in at least one of the most important main lines affected by break of gauge, that from Melbourne, in Victoria, to Sydney, in New South Wales, which will be ready for through traffic as this book goes to press.

Until the British Railways Modernization Plan our own locomotive manufacturers had no big home market for standardized products. Unlike the Americans, they had to find their principal diesel traction markets outside their own country and build locomotives tailored to the special requirements of each customer. They had no proved, standard designs to offer British Railways, and, in consequence, British Railways, since they wished to dieselize as fast as they could to cut operating costs and accelerate their working, had no chance to standardize economically on a few types as the Americans have done and the Germans are doing – at least, not at the start of their dieselization programme. British Railways had little option but to invite all the major British manufacturers to produce their own designs of locomotives in specified power ranges. For two or three years, it was hoped, a comparatively small number of each type would be studied in everyday operating conditions, with the object of determining the basic types suitable for standardization to cover the bulk of B.R. diesel locomotive needs.

Unhappily, B.R. finances took such a turn for the worse in the later 1950s that it was impossible to take a leisurely look at the prototype batches of locomotives. To build up a locomotive fleet as quickly as possible, large repeat orders were placed for most of these designs, some of them before the first examples had barely turned a wheel in traffic. And so, with plans to have over 2,000 main line locomotives in service by the end of 1963, British Railways look like reaching the half-way point of their dieselization programme before their standard types, which were being designed during 1961, are evolved. However, there is a certain amount of standardization of components in the existing designs of different manufacturers; the same Sulzer engine, for example, is employed in the 1,100–1,250 Type '2' diesel-electric locomotives built in B.R. works and by the Birmingham Railway Carriage & Wagon Co.

One of the latest British Railways diesel locomotive types – the Beyer Peacock (Hymek) 1,750 h.p. Type 3 diesel-hydraulic No. D7000 for the Western Region.

British-built diesel railcars 'down under' – a twin-unit constructed by the Birmingham Railway Carriage & Wagon Co., with two Fiat 210 h.p. engines per car, photographed between Wellington and Palmerston North on the New Zealand Railways.

[New Zealand Railways

One important issue British Railways hoped a protracted examination of the prototype diesel locomotives would settle was the most economical power ranges in which to build. Should we follow the early American practice of building mainly medium-powered units and working them in multiple on heavy trains, so that there would be no risk of expensive, high-powered machines finding themselves on duties well below their capacity? An important objection to that idea is that to double or treble the length of the motive power, when working multiple-unit, taxes the platform length at some British main-line stations and may produce a train so long that it blocks part of the layout. It must also be remembered that although a 2,000-h.p. diesel locomotive is priced at about £120,000, two separate 1,000-h.p. locomotives add up to about £150,000 in first cost.

At the start, British Railways did order chiefly locomotives in the medium-power range. There has been some multiple-unit working – the Edinburgh–Aberdeen express service, for example, is worked by 1,160-h.p. locomotives in pairs – but in general the operating inconveniences of this method seem to outweigh the advantages and in the last year or so there has been a noticeable emphasis on higher-powered locomotives. Conspicuously, the Western Region is changing from the 2,200-h.p. 'Warship' to a 2,700-h.p. diesel-hydraulic, mounted on two 6-wheel bogies, which appeared in the autumn of 1961; and the coming standard British Railways Type '4' will be a 2,750-h.p. unit on two 6-wheel bogies, of which Nos. D1500–19 are expected to emerge in 1962.

British Railways classify their main-line diesel locomotives in five types according to power. The only occupants of the 3,000-h.p.-plus, Type '5' range are the English Electric 3,300-h.p. 'Deltics', geared for a 100-m.p.h. maximum speed. Type '4' locomotives run from 2,000 to 2,800 h.p. and are all capable of up to 90 m.p.h. Type '3' covers the 1,500 to 1,750-h.p. locomotives, Type '2', 1,000 to 1,365 h.p. and Type '1', 750 to 1,000 h.p. The big stud of over 1,500 diesel shunters, ranging from 204 to 400 h.p., are not separately classified.

At the time of writing it is the western side of Britain which is being dieselized fastest, with conversion of practically all the principal express services on the Midland and West Coast main

One of the massive 8,500 h.p. gas turbine electric-locomotives of the Union Pacific Railroad, U.S.A. The six-axle tender behind the twin-unit locomotive carries its fuel oil. The diagram below shows the layout of the twin-unit locomotive itself.

KEY

1. Air-brake equipment	8. Auxiliary diesel engine	15. Traction generators	21. Traction motors
2. Driving cab	9. Traction-motor blower	16. Turbine air intake	22. Lubricating-oil tank
3. Auxiliary control	10. Radiator	17. Gas turbine	23. Gearbox
4. Compressor	11. Propulsion control	18. Turbine exhaust	24. Air reservoirs
5. Auxiliary generator	12. Sandbox	19. Power-plant equpiment	25. Diesel fuel tank
6. Braking resistor	13. Excitation control	20. Gas-turbine fuel tender	26. Battery box
7. Generator	14. Generator blower		27. Train control

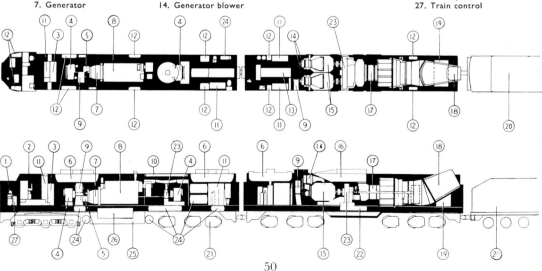

lines of the London Midland Region likely by the end of 1962. By then, too, little steam will be left in the far west of the Western Region's territory in Devon and Cornwall and dieselization should be spreading to the main lines radiating from Bristol. Although diesels are engaged in increasing numbers on the Euston–Crewe main line of the London Midland Region, this is an interim measure pending electrification. The principal arena of dieselization on this Region are the routes from St. Pancras to the Midlands, Leeds and Manchester and from Birmingham to Leeds; on the latter route the London Midland's scheme merges with the North Eastern Region's schemes covering the main lines between Newcastle, York and the West Riding of Yorkshire, and there will probably be a great deal of economical inter-Regional diesel locomotive working. In Scotland, as has already been remarked, the East Coast Route has been dieselized between Edinburgh and Aberdeen and diesels are currently taking over the mountainous routes in the northern part of the country. As for the Eastern Region, the Great Eastern Line's express passenger and freight services will be all but totally dieselized by the end of 1961 and with the arrival of the 'Deltics' steam will take second place on the East Coast Route from London to the North.

Before it commenced dieselization, the Western Region of British Railways experimented with two gas turbine-electric locomotives, one built by Brown Boveri in Switzerland, the other designed and constructed in this country by Metropolitan-Vickers (the latter was converted into British Railways' first 25kV a.c. electric locomotive, No. E2001, for crew-training purposes, in 1958). A gas turbine is very much like a jet engine. It sucks air from the atmosphere; this air is then highly compressed and mixed in a combustion chamber with low-grade fuel oil, sprayed through very fine nozzles. The mixture is ignited and reaches an extremely intense heat, sufficient to expand the hot gases at a velocity of something like 1,500 m.p.h. as they swirl into and rotate the turbine, after which they are exhausted to the atmosphere. In a gas turbine-electric locomotive the turbine shaft drives both the compressor for the incoming air and a generator, which produces current to power electric traction motors on the bogies in the same way as on a diesel-electric traction unit.

Quite apart from technical equipment troubles, the gas turbine-electrics were not ideally suited to British climate and railway traffic conditions. In the first place, a gas turbine locomotive thrives on hard work. When the turbine is on 'full load' – that is, when the locomotive has a job demanding its maximum power output – its thermal efficiency is about three times that of a steam locomotive; in other words, it will do about three times as much work for the same amount of energy extracted from fuel consumed. But when the gas turbine is not required to work full out – when it is on 'part load' – its thermal efficiency is no better than that of a steam engine; since it costs three or four times as much to build and its maintenance costs are substantial, in such conditions the gas turbine locomotive is not a profitable investment. The most powerful of the two Western Region locomotives, the Metropolitan-Vickers product, was only on 'full load' for about 20 per cent of its normal operating life.

On one U.S. railroad operating conditions are much better suited to the gas turbine locomotive's characteristics; this is the Union Pacific, which is the only system in the world to operate gas turbines in quantity. Since 1949 it has bought twenty-five 4,500-h.p. locomotives of this kind and then forty-five 8,000-h.p. machines – monsters of 364 tons' weight that need two close-coupled units to carry all their equipment *and* a bogie oil tank behind for their 24,000-gallon fuel supplies. The Union Pacific locomotives handle freight trains of up to 5,000 tons' weight over a 484-mile section of transcontinental main line between Chicago and San Francisco which climbs to a summit of 8,013ft, twice the height of Scotland's Ben Nevis; in part, this line is steeper than 1 in 100 for 65 continuous miles. On such a gradient and with such loads the gas turbines are always at full stretch and therefore working at peak efficiency; moreover, for technical reasons there is no need to explore here, a turbine functions more efficiently when it takes in the colder air of the higher altitudes of a line like this. Once the Union Pacific gas turbine locomotive has passed the summit, the gas turbine is cut out and the locomotive and train coast economically down the long slope under the control of a powerful braking system.

Where the environment is as ideal for a gas turbine as the Union Pacific's territory, the most is made of its other selling-points. It packs more power per cubic foot into its framework than a diesel locomotive of the same size; even using some of the most powerful diesels now available

A private-venture gas turbine locomotive with mechanical drive to the road wheels, built by English Electric, which went into experimental service on British Railways in 1961. The locomotive is oil-fired.

[*E. N. Bellass*]

to the U.S. railroads, it would need three of them and a bit more besides to equal the output of one of the Union Pacific's 8,500-h.p. gas turbines, and their maintenance costs would be considerably higher per h.p. Finally, the crude oil a gas turbine burns is cheaper than diesel fuel.

One of the snags of the gas turbine locomotives mentioned is that the air compressor takes such a large proportion of the gas turbine's power output. The Swiss-built locomotive of the Western Region, for example, had a gas turbine that developed just over 10,000 h.p.; but three-quarters of that was required to drive the air compressor and only 2,500 h.p. was left for load haulage. Variations of the gas turbine principle, however, have found a way round this objection.

The best-known is the free-piston-gasifier-turbine. A famous firm experimenting with this device for railway purposes is Renault of France, which built a 1,000-h.p. locomotive for trial on French Railways in 1953 and, when this had satisfactorily run over 205,000 miles, followed it in 1960 with a much bigger machine, embodying two turbines and putting out 2,400 h.p. The basis of the free-piston-gasifier is that the compressed air is produced by what is really a normal two-stroke, single-cylinder, opposed piston oil engine independent of the turbine. As the heads of the opposed pistons meet they compress the air, which is mixed with atomized fuel and then ignited in an explosion which hurls the pistons apart again. The other end of each piston drives into a separate cylinder compressing air for the gas turbine's combustion chamber. The power put out by the turbine can be controlled by regulating the amount of oil injected, so as to limit or increase the violence of ignition, and consequently the stroke of the opposed pistons, which in turn lowers or raises the degree of compression of the air supplied to the gas turbine. The Russians and Swedes have also experimented with locomotives operating on similar principles. Most railway experts, however, would be very surprised to see the gas turbine become a serious challenge to the diesel engine as the railways' internal combustion motive power of the 1960s.

III

THE AGE OF ELECTRIFICATION

EARLY in 1954, the French Railways initiated a series of experiments to explore the speed potential of what were then their latest electric locomotives. The French, as always since the war, were looking to the future. They wanted an idea both of the speeds their rolling stock could sustain without detriment to safety and also of the maximum loads the electrical equipment could bear.

For the first trials, they selected a 23-mile stretch of track which was almost dead straight and practically level near Dijon, the big traffic centre on the main line from Paris to Lyons and Marseilles. Then No. CC-7121, a 104-ton, 4,700-h.p. locomotive on two 6-wheel bogies, was attached to a 3-coach train of 111 tons and set to make a series of high speed runs over the test section. From a maximum of 102 m.p.h. on the first trip, speeds were intensified on successive runs, until on February 21, 1954, a new world rail speed record of 151 m.p.h. was notched. At this mark the French rested content for a while; but they had taken careful note that the electric motors of the locomotive had not been pressed to the maximum output of which they were capable.

For any bid to raise the speed record higher than 150 m.p.h., a longer stretch of straight track than the one near Dijon was essential. The French found it on the other side of the country, on the main line from Bordeaux to Hendaye. Now they took out of service a sister of the 151 m.p.h. record-breaker, No. CC-7107, and a newer type evolved since the 1954 exploit, No. BB-9004, an 80-ton, 4,000-h.p. machine on two 4-wheel bogies, to modify them for a still more daring high speed venture. The principal alterations were re-gearing of the drive from the traction motors to the axles to allow for speeds up to 350 m.p.h.; this, calculation had shown to be the theoretical limit at which the motors would blow up. The only other modification of any consequence was the equipment of the two locomotives with special pantographs; and the sole attention paid to the racing track was the realignment of its one slight curve. Rather more attention was given to the 3-coach train made up for the experiments; to reduce air resistance to the minimum, the coaches were stripped of all outside door handles, steps and ventilators, an 8ft long streamlined tail was fitted to the end of the last coach and all three vehicles were air-smoothed from head to tail by the application of rubber sheeting to the gaps between them.

After some 'warm-up' sprints in the lower 'hundreds', No. BB-9004 was opened up to the extent of a new world record of 171½ m.p.h. on March 26, 1955. Thorough examination by the engineers could detect no ill-effects to the train, the electrical equipment or the track, and two days later No. CC-7107 was authorized to make a supreme effort. It was not just the fantastic pace that made her a thrilling spectacle as she raced past 150 m.p.h., for with the strength of current the motors were taking and at this high speed the arcing between the contactors of the locomotive's pantograph and the overhead wire was brilliantly explosive. But at around the 190 m.p.h. mark, the heat generated became so intense that the contactors began to disintegrate. Promptly the driver was ordered to ease up; such was the rate of acceleration even at this unprecedented level of speed, however, that No. CC-7107 had by then crossed the 200 m.p.h. mark to a peak of 205½ m.p.h.

No. BB-9004 was sent out next day to match its predecessor's feat. On this locomotive, unhappily, the contactors began to glow, melt and break up rather earlier, but rather than call off the attempt the engineers on the train quickly decided on a daring move. At 180 m.p.h., with the vicious draught from the racing train blasting the ballast up to window height, the driver was ordered by telephone to lower the ruined pantograph and raise the locomotive's other one. There was a breathless moment; but the change was perfectly executed and No. BB-9004 was able to maintain its acceleration until a further 205½ m.p.h. satisfied the engineers, after which the train was halted.

These French exploits, of course, were startling enough to capture world press headlines. They demonstrated that with electric traction the standard-gauge railways of the world's industrialized nations had the prime moving means to transform their speed of operation to the same extent, proportionally, as jet engines have accelerated air transport. The Americans and the Germans built steam locomotives capable of regular working at 100 m.p.h., but no one has yet suggested that one suitable for twice that pace is a practicable proposition. A 200 m.p.h. diesel locomotive is another matter, but where the electric traction unit scores against this rival is that its primary source of energy is stationary in the power stations which generate the current and the sub-stations which distribute it to the conductors; the diesel unit must carry its power plant on its frames, where the complex mechanism is subject to stresses of travel that are one of the major problems diesel locomotive engineers have to overcome. The length of the electric unit's lead in reliability over diesel traction might be further increased if these stresses were exaggerated in the pursuit of much higher average speeds.

By many less spectacular achievements, the French have demonstrated the all-purpose reliability of electric traction. For example, to test the capacity of the power supply on the Bordeaux–Hendaye line prior to the March, 1955, records, they ran a double-headed, 17-coach train of 725 tons over the test length at 120 m.p.h. In the same year of 1955, another of the 6-axle electric locomotives, No. CC-7147, totted up the fantastic total of 273,400 miles in a little over six months' regular service on the Paris–Dijon–Lyons main line; for 220 days, from May 1 to December 7, it was therefore *averaging* 51·5 m.p.h. incessantly, day in, day out. As recently as the spring of 1961, another French unit, No. BB–20103, was set to average 100 m.p.h. start to stop on a 67-mile test run from Strasbourg to Mulhouse, and maintained 115–118 m.p.h. for 37 miles on end.

Routine French operation is nowadays little below the special standards described in the previous paragraph. Every one of the principal expresses streaming daily up and down the 317·4-mile main line between Paris and Lyons is timed to cover the distance at an average of

One of the earliest types of French Railways a.c. electric loco-motive, whose success did so much to encourage the present-day spread of high voltage a.c. electrification. This 'BB-13000' class seen here at Valenciennes on a Basle–Calais express is now superseded on principal express work by more modern types.

This is the handsome outline of the modern French Railways electric locomotive, used for both 1,500 volts d.c. and 25,000 volts a.c. machines. No. BB–9262 is one of the French d.c. locomotive fleet, leaving Paris for the Spanish border with the 'Sud Express', which every day runs non-stop over the 359·7 miles to Bordeaux at an average of 69·6 m.p.h.

[French Railways

60 m.p.h. or better. From a mile a minute the timings range in pace up to the peak of the 'Mistral', which takes only 143 minutes over the 195·3 miles to Dijon, averaging 81·9 m.p.h. all the way; it is allowed a mere 95 minutes for the next 122·1 miles to Lyons, for an average of 77·1 m.p.h.; and it reaches Marseilles by 8·39 p.m., having averaged 68·4 m.p.h. throughout the 535·4 miles from Paris with four intermediate stops included (and electric haulage only as far as Avignon – 461 miles from Paris).

Two features of this performance need to be emphasized. First, the French expresses on the Lyons main line are not lightweight affairs of half a dozen coaches or so like the British 'Caledonian' or 'Master Cutler'. They are made up consistently to 600 to 800 tons' weight of modern, fully air-conditioned coaches; the 'Mistral', even though it is a first-class-only service, usually conveys 15 or 16 stainless steel cars weighing as much as 750 tons. Second, the timings are not maintained at the cost of a breakneck sprinting downhill. Over a few sections a maximum of 99 m.p.h. is permitted and in some other areas 93 m.p.h., but the ceiling is generally 87 m.p.h. The French take advantage of the unequalled accelerative ability of an electric unit and the fact that almost unlimited power is available on an electrified railway, if one builds traction units with a capacity to employ it. The standard electric locomotive on the Paris–Lyons main line is now an 82-ton, 5,200 h.p. four-axle type capable of working 1,000-ton trains at a steady 90 m.p.h. on level track. At starting, or in recovery from a speed check *en route*, the locomotive makes maximum use of its power to get its train rolling in the 80-m.p.h. range as quickly as possible, assuming that the local track conditions permit these speeds straight away. This achieved, the driver relaxes the supply of current to the motors; and thereafter, he applies his knowledge of the route to skilful use of the controller so that the train's speed stays as nearly constant as possible, whether the road is uphill or down.

The reserve of high power afforded by electrification is demonstrated even more strikingly on the main line from Paris to Lille. Between these two great commercial centres the French Railways operate a high-speed businessmen's service with lightweight trains of no more than five coaches. One of these is currently the fastest train in the world, for over part of its journey it is timed at an average of 84·9 m.p.h.; the distance over which this average is required, however, is a mere 41·1 miles from Arras to Longueau, scheduled in 29 minutes, and over that stretch the maximum speed must not exceed 87·5 m.p.h. If the record-holding train, the 11.45 a.m. from

Lille, is to have any hope of keeping time between Arras and Longueau, therefore, it must employ its full power for acceleration; but a great deal less will suffice to keep the five coaches rolling at the maximum 87·5 m.p.h. once this rate has been reached.

From this discussion of French achievements, the most powerful selling points of electrification are readily apparent. Here are locomotives with more brilliant accelerative powers than anything else on rails and with a higher power-to-weight ratio than the best any diesel manufacturer can devise (note that the 5,200-h.p. continuous output – the maximum is over 7,000 h.p. – of the modern French locomotive is obtained for no more than 82 tons' weight, which is considerably superior to the German diesel-hydraulic achievements described in the last chapter). Their unsurpassed availability for work and the almost negligible amount of time they need to retire from duty each week for servicing is apparent from the endurance feat of the French locomotive in averaging over a thousand miles a day for six months. So much of the electric traction unit's equipment is self-contained, easily accessible and simply installed that it lends itself to a high degree of repair by replacement; that is, faulty assemblies can be repaired at leisure, while the locomotive is quickly returned to traffic with a substitute assembly from store. A factor contributing substantially to this high degree of reliability is that the electric locomotive does not carry with it its primary source of power.

The outcome of an electric traction unit's reliability is that its performance is more accurately predictable than that of any other means of rail haulage. The operators of an electrified railway can trust each locomotive of a class to put up an identical showing with a given load over a specific route, day in and day out: this they could never confidently anticipate from a temperamental steam locomotive, susceptible to vagaries of driving method and maintenance or varying quality of coal, and it is not true of diesel traction to the same extent. The benefit of such consistency to the preparation and execution of a timetable will be obvious. It means that nowadays timetables can be compiled by electronic computers; the compilers can feed into the computer details of the route and its gradients, the stops to be made, the loads of the trains to be worked and the characteristics of the locomotive to haul them, assured that the result will be perfectly practicable schedules.

The proof of more economical traffic operation with electric traction is shown in figures issued by the French Railways at the end of 1960. By this time 17·6 per cent of their total route mileage was electrified, but it was carrying 54 per cent of the system's traffic and needed fewer than 1,500 electric locomotives and 500 electric multiple-units to do it, as compared with a total of over 5,000 steam locomotives prior to electrification. Each electric locomotive was running on the average three times the daily mileage of each French steam locomotive (and French steam locomotives were averaging half as much daily mileage again as those of British Railways). Moreover, thanks to more efficient use of coal in power stations to produce electric current, French Railways had cut their fuel consumption by over a third compared with 1938, even though their passenger traffic had risen by 35 per cent and their freight traffic by 28 per cent in the same period.

So far, the case for electrification seems unassailable. There is, however, one forbidding objection – the cost. The expense of establishing a supply network from power stations to lineside and then the provision of conductors from which the electric trains can take their power is enormous. Before the last war, the electrification of railways, providing a high reserve of traction power at all times, could only be justified where traffic was heavy. Alternatively, a source of natural energy was desirable – in other words, mountainous areas, from which water tumbled in sufficient volume and with power enough to drive power-station turbines; but even where there were possibilities of hydro-electric power, the railways had to take account of the high cost of damming the water in the heights and conducting pipelines down the mountainsides, so that here too a high level of traffic throughout the day was an economic requisite for electrification.

The outstanding example of a country which has exploited hydro-electric resources is Switzerland, where the entire main line railway system is now electrified. The Swiss railways have another great advantage. By virtue of Switzerland's central situation in Europe, its principal main lines are international, so that a great deal of its trunk traffic is hauled from one end of the country to the other; this helps the major Swiss railways to achieve the best financial results in

Above: A 6,000 h.p. class 'Ae6/6' locomotive of the Swiss Federal Railways emerges from the $9\frac{1}{4}$-mile Gotthard Tunnel at Göschenen with an international express from Italy.

[*Swiss Federal Railways*

Right: The southern portal of another of the great Alpine tunnels, the Lötschberg, $9\frac{1}{8}$ miles long. A car ferry service operates through the tunnel.

[*Bern–Lotschberg–Simplon Railway*

Left: Spectacular bridgework is a feature of the Swiss Railways through the Alps. This is the Bietschtal Bridge, carrying the Lötschberg railway on its descent from the passage of the Bernese Oberland mountains into the Rhone valley at Brigue; the main 312 ft span of the 450 ft-long bridge carries the track 255 ft above the bottom of the gorge.

Right: The world's most powerful locomotive is the 8,800 h.p. Type 'Ae8/8' twin-unit which the Lötschberg Railway uses to haul 800-ton freight trains over its Alpine main line.

[*B.L.S.*

To gain height quickly in its conquest of the Alpine passes, the Gotthard line of the Swiss Federal Railways resorts to spiral tunnels in the mountainside. The line in the lower foreground is just plunging into a spiral on the left, from which it emerges at the level on which the freight train is seen; the top end of the freight train is just heading into another spiral tunnel, from which the railway comes out to cross the river Ticino at the lowest level.

Two more views which show dramatically the rugged, mountainous terrain through which the Gotthard engineers had to cut their main line through narrow valleys from the Lake of Lucerne up to the Gotthard Tunnel. The lower picture shows another Swiss Federal class 'Ae6/6' locomotive passing Wassen, where the railway traces two more spirals – and in consequence the little church on the right comes into view three times, to the bewilderment of those passengers who are not aware of the path the railway is taking!

[Swiss Federal Railways

RAILWAYS THROUGH THE ALPS
(Continued)

Europe – and it also increases train-loads that are already heavy, so far as passenger traffic is concerned, because of the superb tourist attractions of Switzerland itself.

Two of Switzerland's main lines linking Western Europe with Italy and the South-East are among the most difficult in the world. One is the Gotthard, which has to climb 2,080ft in the space of 18 miles, necessitating gradients as steep as 1 in 38½ to 1 in 40 for two-thirds of the way, before it dives deep underground in the 9¼-mile Gotthard tunnel.

Up these steep slopes the modern 121-ton, 6,000-h.p., 6-axle Class Ae6/6 electric locomotive of the Swiss Federal Railways maintains a steady 40 to 45 m.p.h. with international trains of 500 tons' weight. The Lötschberg main line, too, is graded almost continuously at 1 in 37 for 11 miles as it fights its way up the Kander Valley to a passage of the Bernese Oberland mountains in the 9⅛-mile long Lötschberg tunnel, after which comes a long and equally precipitous descent into the Rhone valley at Brigue. The latest Lötschberg locomotives weigh no more than 79 tons and have a 1,000-h.p. traction motor on each of their four axles, making a total output of 4,000 h.p.; one of these Type Ae4/4 machines can keep a 400-ton train rolling up the unyielding 1 in 37 at a steady 40 to 45 m.p.h.

Italy is another country whose railways have profited from ample hydro-electric resources; about two-thirds of its trains now run under electric power. The fastest point-to-point rail journey ever recorded in the world still stands to the credit of the Italian Railways – and, thanks to electric traction, it was made over a main line which has to surmount a summit 1,058ft up in the rugged Apennine Mountains. The course was the 195¾ miles from Florence over the mountains to Bologna and on to Milan across the flat Po valley; and the date was July 20, 1939.

The whole distance, two miles farther than from Euston to Liverpool, was completed by a 3-car electric multiple-unit, one of the pioneers of a now extensive Italian fleet of electric train sets, in a shade over 115 minutes, which meant an astonishing start-to-stop average speed of 102 m.p.h. Ten miles out of Florence, at Prato, the main line to Milan begins its assault on the Apennines and for the next 10¾ miles the average gradient is 1 in 106, but the electric unit romped up the long slope at an average of 89¼ m.p.h., without its speed falling below 82 m.p.h. at any point. With speed rising to 99 m.p.h. on slightly easier gradients, it plunged into the 11½-mile long Apennine Tunnel under the crest of the mountains to emerge at 109 m.p.h. for the long, sinuous descent to Bologna. I have travelled this route myself in one of Italy's latter-day luxury multiple-units, to which more detailed reference is made in Chapter IV, and I still marvel at the skill of the driver on that 1939 run in maintaining his stupendous average speed downhill without tempting Providence on the frequent curves.

The route beyond Bologna is more or less flat and excellently aligned for high speeds; here the record-breaking electric train was able to keep speed almost continuously at 100 m.p.h. or over, and in fact for 123¾ miles straight off the reel the average was 109¼ m.p.h., with a maximum of 126 m.p.h. near Piacenza. The progress of today's expresses over this main line is not so hectic, but the Italian Railways have made such a remarkable recovery from their wartime devastation that the speed of the streamlined 'Settebello' between Rome, Florence, Bologna and Milan has for some years been considerably faster than anything British Railways are offering until 1962 over the comparable distance – and much easier route – between London and Edinburgh.

A country in which the high cost of electrification has been justified by the intensity of main-line traffic alone is Japan, where the immensely busy Japanese National Railways carry seven times the volume of passenger traffic and over three times the volume of freight moved by British Railways. This great weight of traffic is handled entirely on 3ft 6in gauge, not our standard 4ft 8½in, and on it the J.N.R. operates the fastest and most stylish narrow-gauge trains in the world. For its length, the Tokyo–Osaka main line is one of the most active in the world, carrying an average of five passenger and goods trains an hour in each direction over the whole distance. But this total is greatly increased by the many trains which do not travel the whole 344 miles, since the route threads through a succession of rapidly expanding heavy industrial areas, serves 36 million people, 40 per cent of Japan's population, connects some 40 cities and accounts for close on a quarter of the total passenger and goods traffic carried by the J.N.R. Moreover, both Tokyo and Osaka each operate one of the world's busiest suburban railway networks; in Tokyo the rush-hour commuter trains are operated at two-minute headways. The close succession of trains of the Tokyo–Osaka main line at most periods of the day is almost incredible; for example,

The German Federal Railway is the world's most extensive operator of battery electric railcars, of several different types. The cars can run for about 180 miles on one battery-charge; the batteries are recharged at suitably appointed terminal stations during the night – a job taking about five hours.

between 8.15 p.m. and 11.40 p.m. no fewer than 20 main-line trains stream out of Tokyo to points over 100 miles distant down the Osaka line – and this total takes no account of the local services.

Population and industry are still multiplying steadily along the route of the Tokyo–Osaka main line and before long it will be completely choked by increased traffic. To enlarge its capacity would incur massive engineering works in the big city areas and the very tiresome widening of 1,000 level crossings. A cheaper course, the Japanese have decided, is to build a brand-new 4ft 8½in gauge 310-mile electric railway between the two cities, the fastest in the world when the Japanese finish it in 1964 or 1965; the first test section was to be ready for operation in 1961. Designed for through inter-city traffic, it is being laid out for maximum speeds of 155 m.p.h. by passenger trains, which will be scheduled to complete the 310 miles in about three hours, and 93 m.p.h. by goods trains. To allow for the shock of two trains passing at a combined speed of 300 m.p.h., its two tracks are being laid wider apart than usual and the tunnels will be as high from the floor to roof as a three-storey building.

The new railway will be operated exclusively by multiple-unit trains, on which the train

A three-car electric multiple-unit of the German Federal Railway for suburban service between Stuttgart and Nuremberg.

weight can be distributed more evenly than on locomotive-hauled trains, to permit the high speeds envisaged without unduly increasing the construction and maintenance costs of the permanent way; moreover the adhesion of multiple-units will be better, giving the civil engineers more freedom with gradients in laying out the line. Passenger trains will be made up of 4-car units, each of which will be powered with traction motors on every axle, and freight trains of 10-car units, in each of which four cars will have each axle motored. Freight traffic will be carried entirely in containers, of which each 10-car unit will be able to carry 50; the Japanese intend these express container freight trains to cover the 310 miles of the new line between Tokyo and Osaka in a mere $5\frac{1}{2}$ hours. The remaining goods traffic will continue to use the old 3ft 6in gauge line between the two cities.

There will be another important difference between the old and the new Tokyo–Osaka lines, apart from the gauge. Like 95 per cent of J.N.R. electrification, the old line operates on 1,500 volts direct current; the new line will work on 20,000 volts alternating current – in other words, its new high speed multiple-units will be taking current untransformed from the country's industrial supply network. The technical improvements in high voltage a.c. electrification have had a far greater significance for the world railways than any other development since the war; not only have they improved still further the performance of electric traction, but more important, they have cheapened the first cost of electrification, making it economically practicable for lines whose level of traffic might have been considered inadequate to justify conversion previously. The pioneers in this technical progress have been the French, who similarly employed 1,500 volts d.c. to spread their electrified network south of Paris (which includes the Paris–Lyons–Marseilles route), but who are assiduously and speedily developing a 25,000 volts a.c. network in the thriving industrial area to the north and east of their capital based on the Paris–Lille–Strasbourg triangle and the main lines from Paris to the Belgian frontier.

In the early days of electrification, railways were content with comparatively low voltages that were adequate to work light trains over fairly short distances. Thus the Southern Region of British Railways is still building on the 660 volts d.c. system with third-rail conductors originated by the London & South Western Railway, later absorbed into the Southern Railway, for its London suburban services. At this low pressure, which is being raised slightly to 750 volts in today's S.R. extensions, a third rail can be used as a conductor, the current returning through the running rails or, on some systems, through a fourth rail. But most major railway systems deemed a high voltage to be essential for heavy long-distance haulage; and with the higher voltages, overhead wire conductors are essential for safety and more economical.

In 1910 electrical engineering developments enabled the Berne–Lötschberg–Simplon Railway of Switzerland to adopt a 15,000-volts a.c. overhead electrification system at a frequency of $16\frac{2}{3}$ cycles per sec. – that is to say, current completing $16\frac{2}{3}$ cycles of alternation per second. Current produced for general industrial and national supply purposes is normally of 50-cycle frequency. The Swiss chose the lower frequency because it simplified the design of traction motor on their locomotives, and in their country rich with hydro-electric resources the provision by the railway of its own power stations to supply $16\frac{2}{3}$-cycle current would not be an intolerable financial burden. The great advantage of using a high-voltage supply on which the Swiss were intent was that it would economise substantially in the number of sub-stations necessary to feed the current to the overhead wires, for reasons we shall discuss shortly.

The Swiss example was later followed by Germany, Austria, Norway and Sweden, and in the U.S.A. by the Pennsylvania and New Haven railroads. But the majority of the world's railways pursuing electrification before 1939 adhered to the d.c. method, at voltages from 1,500 to 3,000. Local considerations usually counted for more in the choice of system than any thought of future through running. For example, the Belgians, with the Dutch and French 1,500 volts d.c. and the German 15,000 volts a.c. networks close at hand, went odd man out and selected a 3,000-volts supply system, simply because the average distance between their principal junctions was the same as that desirable between sub-stations with 3,000 volts d.c.

Besides Belgium, the principal practitioners of 3,000 volts d.c. are Brazil, Italy, whose achievements have been mentioned, Spain and South Africa. South Africa's coastline surrounds a vast central plateau some 5,000ft above sea level, ringed by ranges of mountains that run down almost to the seashore itself. The difficulty of the terrain persuaded the railway builders of old to adopt

3ft 6in gauge and in more recent years it has been a great inducement to the South African engineers to extend the country's electrified network, which now totals 1,200 route miles.

Even after 1945, the first post-war French and British electrifications were carried out on the 1,500 volts d.c. system. The British line converted was the one over the Pennines from Sheffield to Manchester. In recent years the decline in the British coal trade has deprived this scheme of some of its virtue, but at the time of its completion it was a classic example of a difficult but heavily trafficked route that both profited from and made profit of electrification. The former L.N.E.R. main line strikes uphill from Sheffield with nearly 19 miles of continuous climbing at 1 in 120 to 135 into the Pennines, where it plunges into the 3-mile long Woodhead Tunnel, and then drops at 1 in 100 to 122 for 9 miles towards Manchester. The use of 88-ton, 1,800 h.p. electric locomotives has almost halved the time needed to drag heavy hauls of South Yorkshire coal over the summit to Lancashire industry; moreover, because they take so much less time over each journey, the locomotive force itself has been practically halved by comparison with the days of steam, effecting a considerable economy in train crewmen.

Restraining their trains on the descent from the Pennines, the electric locomotives even restore some of the current they have consumed on the climb to Woodhead Tunnel, for they are equipped with two additional forms of braking that are possible with electric traction motors and which economize considerably in wear and tear on the conventional mechanical braking apparatus. The first is regenerative braking, whereby the electric traction motors are turned into generators, so that they exert a resistance to the momentum of the train and the current thus produced is fed back into the supply system. When this method loses some of its effectiveness below 15 m.p.h., rheostatic braking switches the current supply generated by the traction motors from the overhead wires to resistances in the locomotive, wherein the current is dissipated as heat.

While the Manchester–Sheffield electrification was reaching completion, however, the French were continuing experiments with still higher voltage a.c. electrification that had been initiated by the Germans before the war on a line in the Black Forest, the Höllental Railway. The Höllental Railway fell in the French Occupation Zone after the war and soon absorbed the interest of French railway engineers. They returned home and in the Aix-les-Bains area of their own country converted a section of line to work on 25,000-volt, 50-cycle frequency a.c. supply from the national electricity network. Their experience convinced many of the world's railways, including British Railways, that the future lay with a.c. electrification. Advances in electrical engineering technique had by now removed the objections to employing 50-cycle current that had decided earlier a.c. electrifiers to use 16⅔-cycle supplies.

A voltage of this magnitude cannot be employed in traction motors of convenient size for railway locomotives and multiple-units and the latter must therefore carry on their frames their own transformers, to step down the voltage after it has been picked up from the overhead wires by their pantographs and before it is fed to the traction motors. Initially, the French attempted to use the transformed current in a.c. motors, but encountered considerable problems. There is within an a.c. motor a tendency for undesirable stray currents to be set up which are exaggerated if a supply at the 50-cycle frequency is used – one of the reasons for past choices of the 16⅔-cycle frequency. There are means of overcoming this disadvantage of the a.c. motor and a great deal of research is being pursued in the hope of making its use practical, but at present the remedies necessitate a traction motor of larger size than is desirable and most railway electrical engineers still prefer to employ d.c. traction motors. For this reason early 16⅔-cycle a.c. locomotives had their big traction motors mounted on the main frames of the locomotive, instead of compactly on the bogies as is customary in modern practice; the drive was taken from the motor to large-size driving-wheels by a jackshaft and side coupling-rods similar to those of a steam locomotive. On the Swiss Federal Railways and in Sweden, to quote two examples, one can still find main-line locomotives of this character at work.

Before a.c. can be fed to d.c. motors, it must be rectified; and in the past the bulk and cost of the mechanically-operated convertors that had to be mounted on each traction unit to change the current supply from a.c. to d.c. was a powerful objection to an a.c. system; but now the current can be rectified without the use of any mechanical device. Today's British or French 3,000–5,000-h.p. a.c. locomotive can carry its own transformer and rectifier without exceeding 80 tons in weight. Moreover, these new-style rectifiers can be designed to fit snugly beneath the

BRITISH ELECTRIC TRAINS

Right: On the 25,000 volts a.c. Crewe - Manchester electrification – G.E.C.-built 3,300 h.p. locomotive No. E3038 speeds through Holmes Chapel with the 7.10 a.m. Birmingham–Manchester Piccadilly express.

[*B. S. Jennings*

Above: A four-car multiple-unit of the 25,000 volts a.c. Manchester-Crewe scheme arrives at Crewe.

[*M. Mensing*

Above: One of the blue-liveried 25,000 volts a.c. Glasgow suburban electric trains, built by Pressed Steel, at Hyndland.

[*W. A. C. Smith*

Right: Class 'EM1' 1,870 h.p. electric locomotive No. 26047 descends from the Pennines with a southbound freight on the 1,500 volts d.c. Manchester-Sheffield electrified line.

[*K. Field*

Left: This 258-ton, articulated three-unit locomotive with an unusual ID+D+DI wheel arrangement and jackshaft and coupling rod drive to the road wheels (*see page 62*) has an output of 7,500 h.p. and was built for heavy iron ore haulage in the far north of the Swedish State Railways' 15,000 volts a.c. electrified system.

Above: The express train speeds of the Swedish State Railways are quite smart. This Swedish-built 3,300 h.p., lightweight locomotive heading the 'Gothenburger' covers the 285 miles between Gothenburg and Stockholm in $4\frac{1}{2}$ hrs, inclusive of one intermediate stop, and averages better than a mile a minute for 195 miles of its journey.

Below: A feature of the Swedish State Railways' new close coupled three-car multiple-units, called the 'Paprika trains' because of their bright red livery with white stripes, is their ability to be coupled or uncoupled in a matter of minutes into two-, three- or four-car formations.

[Swedish State Railways

British Railways 3,300 h.p. 25kV a.c. electric locomotive No. E3001, built by Associated Electrical Industries (Rugby)

[Blocks courtesy of Locomotive & Allied Manufacturers Association]

British Railways 1,000 h.p. Type 'I' diesel-electric mixed traffic locomotive
No. D8000, built by English Electric

[Blocks courtesy of English Electric Co.

frames of a multiple-unit motor coach, so that no passenger or luggage-carrying space is sacrificed. Two kinds of rectifier have been adopted for the modern a.c. traction unit. One is the mercury-arc rectifier, of either the excitron or ignitron kind, and the other the semi-conductor or transistor variety, incorporating a material such as silicon or germanium; the effect in each case is the same – to allow the current to flow only in one direction.

The advantages of employing a high-voltage feed at the industrial frequency begin with the obvious one that the supply can be taken direct from the national grid system. Next, since the power derived from electricity is a multiple of its voltage and current, in a high-voltage system the overhead wires need to carry less current to meet the peak demands of traction units on heavy trains; moreover, there is a much higher reserve of power in the overhead network to satisfy abnormal demands. If a conductor wire does not have to carry so much current, it can be lighter, thereby saving substantially in the cost of expensive copper for the wires and permitting lighter and cheaper con-

Close-up of an electric locomotive traction motor; it is being fitted to a driving axle of one of the 3,300 h.p. 25,000 volts a.c. electric locomotives built by A.E.I. for British Railways.

[*Associated Electrical Industries (Manchester)*]

ductor supports. The higher the voltage, the farther the current will travel from its point of supply before dropping below efficiency level. The result is that a high-voltage a.c. electrification needs only about a sixth of the sub-stations to distribute the current over a lengthy main line, such as that from Euston to Crewe on British Railways, as would be required for a low voltage d.c. electrification. This was a major inducement to the early pioneers of 15,000-volt, $16\frac{2}{3}$-cycle electrification; it increases in importance with still higher voltages. In turn, these advantages significantly reduce the first cost of installing the electrical supply system.

In one important respect the need to transform the current during its passage from the overhead pickup to the traction motors enhances the performance characteristics of an a.c. traction unit, but to understand this we must first examine briefly the working of an electric locomotive. The full traction supply voltage cannot be applied to the traction motors when the locomotive or multiple-unit is at rest and in such conditions it must be stepped down. In a d.c. traction unit this is achieved through resistances, which reduce the voltage to safe levels at the traction motor terminals. As the traction unit accelerates, however, its motors develop a reverse generating or electromotive force, known as 'back e.m.f.', in opposition to the supply voltage. Now the driver can 'notch up' his controller handle, cutting out the resistances one by one until the power circuit is completely free of them, and all the time keeping an eye on his driving desk ammeter, which indicates continuously the amount of current the motors are taking.

Additionally, the supply of current to the motors is controlled by alteration of their grouping, the amount of variation possible being dependent upon the number of the unit's traction motors and the voltage at which they are arranged to work. At starting and when speed is low, the traction motors will be connected in series with all resistances in circuit, so that the voltage is divided equally among all motors. When all the resistances have been cut out and the motors are developing a 'back e.m.f.' so strong that it balances the incoming current supply and further acceleration is impossible, the next stage is to regroup the motors in series-parallel, once more

E

Australian electric multiple-unit – a stainless steel four-car unit
employed on the Sydney-Lithgow 1,500 volts d.c. line of the New
South Wales Government Railways.
[Department of Railways N.S.W.

with all resistances in circuit, so that the voltage is divided equally between each half of the traction motor grouping. Again, the resistances are gradually eliminated. Finally, there may be a parallel grouping, initiated as before with all resistances in circuit, in which each motor takes the full supply voltage. Beyond the last stage of notching up in parallel grouping there may be an arrangement for 'field-weakening', whereby the magnetic fields of the traction motors are lowered in strength in order to reduce the 'back e.m.f.' and permit more current to be fed to the motor, so as to achieve acceleration still higher. On a modern electric traction unit all these sequential adjustments of the resistances and regroupings of the traction motors take place automatically in accordance with the driver's adjustment of his controller, which may have as many as 30 or more notches and additionally one or two stages of field-weakening. On a modern multiple-unit even the rates of acceleration are automatically controlled, so that the driver has only to select the one suitable to the conditions in which he is running or to achieve the final speed he desires. Such practice is convenient with trains of unvarying power/weight ratio, but with a locomotive the choice is usually left to the driver, for his own judgment in relation to the kind and weight of train he is working, although some types have automatic acceleration control.

The methods of current limitation during the starting and acceleration of a d.c. traction unit outlined in the previous paragraph have the disadvantage that if one pair of driving-wheels begins to slip, the slip may spread to others as the distorted current supply passes through each motor in succession while they are grouped in series. With an a.c. locomotive, on the other hand, the speed and torque of the traction motors can be governed by varying the voltage input, and

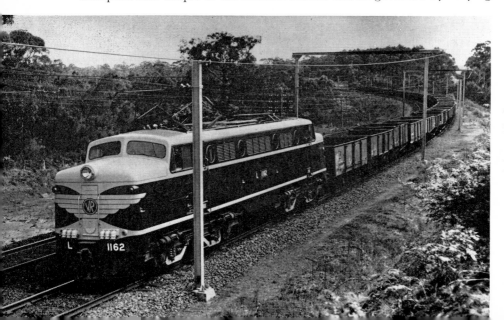

Australian electric loco-
motive – this is one of the
2,400 h.p. locomotives
built in Britain by English
Electric for the Victorian
Government Railways,
which also uses the 1,500
volt d.c. system.
[Victorian Government Railways

marrying the controller notches to a number of different tappings on the transformer. An independent current feed to each traction motor becomes possible and the motors can be connected permanently in parallel, ruling out any possibility of a sympathetic slip of driving axles. The outcome is greatly improved adhesion at starting, the practical effect of which has been demonstrated in some remarkable French experiments with a.c. locomotives, such as the firm restart of a 2,400-ton load by a 124-ton, six-axle locomotive on a curving 1 in 100 incline.

In the bigger countries of the world, where busy main lines cross vast expanses of open territory that are not beset by a close sequence of built-up and heavily industrialized areas, as are those of British Railways, there are few complications to offset the immeasurable advantages of high voltage a.c. electrification following the technical advances of recent years. Thus the U.S.S.R., which previously operated some 3,000 volts d.c. mileage, has now embarked upon a most ambitious 25,000 volts a.c. programme. The whole 3,375-mile western section of the historic Trans-Siberian Railway from Moscow to Lake Baikal is now electrically worked by these methods and

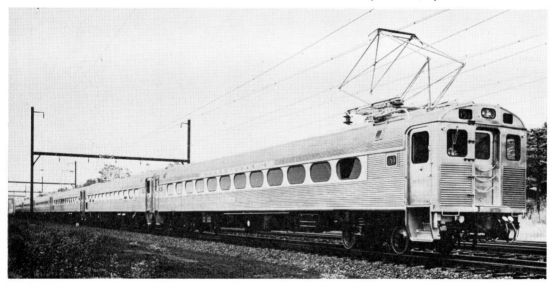

The latest in American electric multiple-units – this Pennsylvania Railroad train is a special lightweight design by the Budd Company, using plastic extensively in the interior layout; the bogies are of particularly novel design with no outside frames and a combination of air and coil springing.

by 1971 the Russians hope to have converted the remaining 2,600 miles or so to Vladivostock, on the Pacific coast. Other routes scheduled for a.c. electrification include the 400-mile main line from Moscow to Leningrad.

The Chinese, too, have elected for the 25,000 volts a.c. system and have finished their first section of 56 miles, covering a line which attacks a 4,560ft summit with a $16\frac{3}{4}$-mile climb of an unbroken 1 in 33 on one side and a $25\frac{1}{2}$-mile ascent at 1 in 50 to the other. This is in the mountains of Central China where there are rich sources of minerals and natural power for the country's great industrialization programme; ultimately the Chinese plan a 25,000 volts a.c. network, embracing this district and the environs of Peking.

By their post-war lead in 25,000 volts a.c. development, the French have won the lion's share of the equipment of similar systems abroad. For example, the success of the locomotives the French firm of Alsthom built for their own home railways has secured orders from China and the U.S.S.R. For the Chinese, Alsthom has produced a 135-ton, 6,300-h.p. 6-axle locomotive that is capable of working 1,500-ton trains up the vicious inclines described in the previous paragraph. The 50 6,000-h.p. locomotives the French firm has delivered to the Soviet Railways are basically similar, except that 10 of them are geared to a maximum speed of 100 m.p.h. for passenger working.

In Western Europe, at least, nations are drawing closer together economically as well as politically, and through railway working is increasing. It might be thought that some railway systems would pause before adopting a new electrification method that would not be compatible with their neighbours, and might therefore hamper the operation of through trains. Nowadays, however, the widest differences in electrification methods seem to have no terrors for the engineers. This year the Swiss have introduced their new 'Trans-Europe Express' units, the first in the 'T.E.E.' scheme with straight electric propulsion, which function without difficulty under four different current systems in their journeys between Paris and Milan. From Milan to Domodossola, near the Swiss–Italian border, they take their current from the Italian 3,000-volts d.c. system; across Switzerland they run on 15,000 volts a.c.; from the Franco–Swiss frontier station of Vallorbe as far as Dôle they encounter one of the French 25,000-volt a.c. stretches; and at Dôle they enter French 1,500-volt d.c. territory for the remainder of their run to Paris. The control system makes the changes in current selection entirely automatic, so that the motormen from the different countries the 'T.E.E.' trains pass through drive the 5-car Swiss train exactly as they would a unit of their own railways. These Swiss 'T.E.E.' trains are capable of a maximum of 100 m.p.h. and this speed potential, coupled with their facility for through running, has revolutionized journeys between Milan and Paris; previously the fastest service available required a little under 10 hours, because of the need for locomotive changes, but now the 511 miles take only eight hours. Over the 195·3 miles between Paris and Dijon, incidentally, the Swiss 'T.E.E.' averages more than 80 m.p.h. throughout. The Germans and French now have electric locomotives capable of working freely on their respective 15,000-volts, $16\frac{2}{3}$-cycle and 25,000-volts, 50-cycle systems which overlap in the Saar; and 2-car multiple-units ply between Amsterdam and Brussels running with equal facility under the Dutch 1,500-volts and Belgian 3,000-volts d.c. overhead wires.

High-voltage a.c. electrification on British Railways faces problems not encountered to the same extent anywhere else in the world where this method has been adopted so far. A disadvantage of the high-voltage a.c. system is that its overhead wires require more substantial clearances than those of a low-voltage d.c. system. We are proud that Britain was the birthplace of railways; but we are also paying for being the early pioneers, as in general the 19th-century builders of our railways had no conception of the size to which their puny inventions were capable of development by latter-day engineers and left little overhead or trackside margin in their structures for enlargement of rolling stock. Some other countries, particularly the United States, were more far-sighted. To secure the more liberal clearances required by modern a.c. electrification, British Railways must enlarge almost every overbridge and carry out major surgical works on most tunnels. This is even more of a burden because our country is so heavily built up and industrialized, so that our bridges are thicker on the ground per route mile, say, than in France; for example, in the whole Euston–Crewe, Manchester and Liverpool electrification scheme no fewer than 750 bridges must be reconstructed to provide the higher clearance essential for 25,000 volts, quite apart from the tunnels which must have their tracks lowered for the same reason, or else be opened up completely, as they have been at Stockport, whereas the 407 route miles of the current Eastern Region electrification of the French Railways, traversing less densely populated countryside, involve the rebuilding of only 220 bridges.

Not only have British Railways more civil engineering work of this kind to do, but less time to do it than their French neighbours. In this instance, too, we are to some extent paying the price of the early spread of our railways. The French run longer and heavier trains, especially freight, than we can, because many of our stations, yards and loops have not the capacity to accommodate them; the French therefore need fewer trains per day to carry their traffic. Moreover, it is a British Railways tradition to offer a frequent passenger service at more or less regular intervals throughout each week-day, whereas the continentals are used to grouping their trains at morning, midday and evening peak periods, which give them lengthy interludes every day during which the engineers can carry out some of their work. In this country the civil and electrical engineers have to tackle any week-day work in the teeth of an almost continuous train service with few equals for intensity anywhere else in the world.

Within British city areas it would be intolerably expensive either to increase the clearances of the profusion of bridges, or else to lower the track to create more headroom for the overhead wires. Unlike other present-day practitioners of 25,000 volts a.c. electrification, British Railways included a great deal of suburban electrification in their early schemes, which involves them in this problem to a greater degree than any other a.c. electrified railway so far. The British solution in such areas as the centre of the Glasgow suburban a.c. scheme and the inner district of the Eastern Region's North-East London network, has been to reduce the voltage to 6,250, for which much less liberal overhead clearances are necessary. The British Railways a.c. electric locomotives and multiple-units are fitted with a device that automatically rearranges the traction unit's equipment to suit the voltage of the conductors under which it is running. At each change-over point between 6,250 and 25,000 volts there is a lineside permanent magnet of the kind used in the B.R. automatic warning system (A.W.S.), described in Chapter VII; the presence of this magnet is detected by a receiver mounted on the bogies of the locomotives and multiple-units, and the reaction of the receiver to the magnet actuates the traction units' automatic changeover device. The need to employ two voltages is a nuisance, the snags of which had some bearing on the disastrous a.c. traction equipment failures that beset the Glasgow multiple-units and some of the North-East London train sets in the early days of both these newly electrified services.

To derive the maximum benefit from the greater availability for work of electric traction units and their higher speed potentialities, the already intensive British main-line services are to be increased in frequency. This means extensive work on the track itself, and the re-designing of

A new age of international railway working is beginning in Europe with the development of electric locomotives able to work on differing voltages. Here are dual-voltage locomotives of the French Railways (*left*) and the German Federal Railway (*right*) at Metz, each capable of working on the French 25,000 volts and the German 15,000 volts a.c. systems.

[*La Vie du Rail*

important stations at focal junctions to facilitate traffic operation. Major civil engineering works in the London Midland Region's Euston–Manchester and Liverpool electrification, for example, have been the creation of a new Manchester Piccadilly station out of the city's old London Road, the rebuilding of Stafford, Birmingham New Street and Wolverhampton High Level stations, and the erection of fly-over junctions at Bletchley and Rugby.

The signalling, unless it is of recent installation, usually requires modernization and modification to suit the running characteristics of the new traction. Quite apart from this, track circuits and other electric signalling apparatus must in any case be altered to prevent interference from the high voltage that might dangerously disrupt their efficiency, and signalling and telecommunications cables must be protected. The immense amount of signalling work involved in 25,000 volts a.c. electrification has proved to be one of the greatest problems facing British Railways in its modernization programme.

All in all, therefore, it is little wonder that the first stages of 25,000 volts a.c. electrification on British Railways have appeared protracted by comparison with progress in France. They have been bedevilled, too, by Government indecision over completion of the Euston–Manchester and Liverpool scheme, the effect of which was to bring a great deal of the work on extension southward from Crewe to a full stop during 1960. Early in 1961 the Government lifted its embargo, but its interference means that we shall not see full electric working between London and the two Lancashire cities until 1966, even though the experience gained by British engineers in the first a.c. schemes has developed techniques that should accelerate the later stages of conversion.

When the work is finished, the West Coast main line should be transformed with a much more frequent and faster service than hitherto – 122 minutes has been spoken of as a standard non-stop timing for the 158 miles from Euston to Crewe. The London Midland Region envisages an hourly interval pattern of multiple-units between Euston, Birmingham and Wolverhampton. Manchester, too, will have a train to and from London every hour, routed alternately via Crewe and Stoke; and each hour there will be a departure from Birmingham for either Manchester or Liverpool, which will connect at Crewe with the fast trains from London to give the Midlands an hourly service to both Manchester and Liverpool. Compared with today's three, there will be four fast day services each way between London and Glasgow, two in the morning and two in the afternoon. Yes, the London Midland electrification, regrettably late in completion though it will be, should be well worth the lengthy period of waiting.

IV

LUXURY PASSENGER TRAINS OF THE WORLD

THE urge to travel has developed enormously since the last war. It has been calculated that since as recently as 1951 the mileage of all inland travel in Britain has risen by a quarter; and other Western European countries could tell a similar story. Unfortunately, the railways have not won a proportionate share of the increase. In Britain, the chief means of inland transport is the private car, motor-cycle or 'moped', which together account for just on half the mileage we travel annually; in the past decade they have doubled their use. Inland British air travel, too, has surged ahead since 1951 and is now running at about treble its volume then, whereas British Railways' increased pickings from the post-war travel boom total a mere 8 per cent. The railways' share of the total inland travel market in this country, although it is now less than a sixth of the total, is still vastly in excess of the air lines' loadings; but with continuing cuts in air fares and the advent of still more efficient high-capacity aircraft, the present situation leaves no room for complacency. What has happened in North America will be repeated here, unless passenger services are progressively revitalized.

The last year in which the revenue from U.S. passenger train operations covered the direct costs of their operation – that is, excluding from the reckoning expenses like track and signalling which they share with freight trains – was 1953. Now direct costs are about £50 million above income; and if all costs, direct *and* indirect, are considered, U.S. passenger trains are losing their operators some £170 million annually or worse. The depths were reached in 1957 with a total loss of close on £260 million. One system alone, the Pennsylvania, has been dropping as much as £37 million a year on its purely passenger train operation. These huge deficits can be tolerated by many railroads because in general their freight carryings greatly outweigh passengers; in a year, for example, the Pennsylvania moves about five-eighths of the freight tonnage worked by British Railways, but only a twentieth of the latter's passengers – moreover, on an average the Pennsylvania runs each ton of its freight nearly four times as far as B.R. But there are important U.S. systems which no longer run a single passenger train; and several others – even up to the mighty New York Central – which would like to follow their example, if they could cut quickly through the red tape which demands legal authority for the severance of service. A Governmental inquiry of 1958 into U.S. long-distance rail passenger operation predicted that if the decline in patronage of the previous ten years persisted at the same rate, the American passenger train would be an item of transport history by 1970.

The principal – though not the only – reason for the woes of U.S. passenger train operators is competition on a scale unknown elsewhere in the world. The U.S.A. is a huge country with some horribly congested big cities, but great, open mileages between them which have helped to make the automobile as natural a piece of American family equipment as the kitchen sink; the nation has 55 million of them to serve a population of 170 million. More important, the size of the country has encouraged a tremendous growth of internal air services, which are the railroads' chief competitors for long-distance and city-to-city passengers. It is Chicago, not New York, which has the busiest airport in the world, because it is the hub of so many purely American civil air operations.

U.S. railroads have done their best to compete by speed. In recent years a Government regulating body, the Inter-State Commerce Commission, has lowered the high standards of some lines by putting a ceiling on speeds where certain forms of automatic train control are not installed, but in total the U.S.A. still leads the world. Every day nearly 300 trains are booked to run over 18,000 miles at averages of 70 m.p.h. or better and some 1,200 travel over 67,000

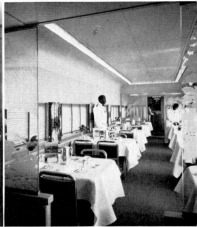

The accommodation of a luxury U.S. transcontinental express would do credit to a first-class hotel. The first picture (*top left*) shows the comfort of 'coach' class travel, the equivalent of European second class, with every seat adjustable to a reclining position; notice the passenger in the background descending from one of the 'Empire Builder's' domes. The coffee shop-lounge car of the 'Empire Builder' (*above centre*) is called the 'Ranch' and is styled with timbered walls and leather upholstery to suit its name. The width of U.S. stock is evident in the view of the 'Empire Builder's' dining car (*top right*).

[*Great Northern Railway*

THE
'EMPIRE BUILDER'
of the
GREAT NORTHERN
RAILWAY, U.S.A.

(see also page 2)

The most eye-catching vehicle in the 'Empire Builder's' make-up is the 'Great Dome' (*above*). On the lower level of this car is an attractive lounge bar (*below left*); the whole of the upper floor is given over to a glass-roofed dome (*below right*) from which 75 passengers have a magnificent panoramic view of the scenery from deep armchairs.

[*Great Northern Railway*

miles daily at 65 m.p.h. or better. One of the most remarkable American services, although it is among those lately dimmed by some deceleration, is that offered by three competing railroads between Chicago and the Twin Cities of Minneapolis and St. Paul, 418 miles distant; in their heyday of the mid-1950s all 16 principal expresses *averaged* 64·8 m.p.h., stops included, throughout this distance and included 26 daily start-to-stop bookings at over 75 m.p.h., the maximum being a still unexcelled 86·2 m.p.h. over one 54·6 m.p.h. section made twice daily by the Burlington Lines' 'Twin Cities Zephyrs'. But although no daily train in the world has yet beaten the 'Twin Cities Zephyr's' onetime best of 86·2 m.p.h., its average is now down to 78·7 m.p.h. over the stretch concerned; at the time of writing the Santa Fe's combined transcontinental 'Super Chief-El Capitan' train tops the U.S. list with an 82·1 m.p.h. average over the 99·9 miles from Garden City to Lamar.

But no rail speeds yet envisaged can outdo a Boeing or Convair jet and U.S. railroads continue to pin a great deal of faith in the counter-attraction of long-distance luxury standards and a variety of travel amenities that make an airliner's cramped saloon a bleak prospect by comparison. Of course, if you are travelling the length or breadth of the U.S.A. or Canada it is more than a day's journey by the fastest express and the train must carry all the facilities of an hotel. Look, for example, at the sleek green and orange, gold-lettered 'Empire Builder' of the Great Northern, a railroad which still holds that 'the world judges the railways by their passenger services' and styles its crack transcontinental trains to match this theory. It is 2,210 miles from Chicago to Seattle, on the Pacific Coast, by the 'Empire Builder', which takes 43 hours 50 minutes to complete the journey and is two nights on the road; on the way it has one sprint of 112½ miles at an average of 72·5 m.p.h. (over the Chicago–St. Paul race-track previously mentioned, by the way, where it uses the Burlington Lines' route; the Great Northern's own territory begins at St. Paul).

In the summer season the 'Empire Builder' loads to 15 cars, which cost the Great Northern £1¼ million to build and equip. Because of the length of the journey, five train sets are needed to provide a daily service, so that this express represents an investment of over £6 million in rolling stock. At the same moment that one streamliner is leaving Union Station in Chicago, a second 'Empire Builder' arrives at this Eastern U.S. terminus from faraway Seattle. Meanwhile, a third train is speeding westward across the Great Plains towards the towering front range of the Montana Rockies. The fourth 'Empire Builder', having arrived that same morning at the seaport city of Seattle, is being readied for its return departure, just 3½ hours away; while back in the vast wheatlands and cattle country of Montana, the fifth 'Empire Builder', also Chicago-bound, nears the half-way point of its two-day journey.

The customary length of a U.S. passenger car is 85ft, so that with a pair of 2,400-h.p. diesel-electric units working in multiple at the front end each 'Empire Builder' train is just over a quarter of a mile long when it leaves Chicago. (On later stages of the run up to four diesel units in multiple will be necessary to surmount the gradients in the Montana Rockies.) The 15 cars on their own tot up to about 1,150 tons, whereas a British 15-coach train would weigh in the region of 500 tons, but these 15 vehicles provide accommodation for no more than 323 passengers; and to serve the 323 travellers the train employs no fewer than 25 staff, including the locomotive crew. 'Manager' of this hotel on rails is the train conductor, whose authority extends even to the driver and fireman, with whom he communicates by telephone. Twenty-five additional trained personnel comprise his staff, including a brakeman, two coach porters, two stewards, five chefs, six waiters, a lounge-car attendant, a Pullman conductor, six sleeping-car porters and a railroad passenger department representative.

Reading from the front, the 'Empire Builder's' make-up begins with a mail and express parcels car, then a baggage-dormitory car which includes 21 bunks for the train staff and a train stewards' room. Next comes a 'coach' – the U.S. equivalent of our second class – for short-distance passengers using the train between its intermediate stops, followed by three more cars in which the seats are adjustable to a reclining position. Reclining seats are now a standard feature of 'coaches' employed on the long-distance U.S. trains involving night travel.

The last three cars are something more than 'coaches' pure and simple. In the centre of their frames they have their floors raised to provide what is now a popular feature – and selling-point – of U.S. long-distance rail travel, the 'Vista-Dome'. Above the 24 seats in this elevated, central part of each car the roof 'blisters' in a long, glazed cupola, so that 'dome' passengers have a sweeping bird's-eye view not only above their heads and to right and left, but to front and rear over the roofs of the train. The Baltimore & Ohio Railroad, incidentally, used to fit its 'domes' with swivelling searchlights to pick out the scenery for their passengers after dark; and a privately owned Japanese railroad, which has lately invested in an electric streamliner with a 'dome', now does the same. In Europe, the only 'domes' to be seen so far are on some French railcars specially designed for scenic routes, but they may appear soon on the 'Rheingold Express' from the Hook of Holland to Cologne, Basle, Switzerland and Italy.

Many North American systems have allowed their designers free rein in fancy décor for their refreshment cars. The 'Empire Builder's' buffet-lounge, the next vehicle we come to, has been trimmed inside to represent a plushy log cabin, with oak-faced walls, 'cedar-log' pillars and leather upholstery, and is named 'The Ranch'. Open all the daylight hours of the journey, from about 6.30 a.m. to late at night, the 'Ranch' offers drinks, snacks and less lavish meals for the traveller on a budget; a lunch of soup, pork chops and vegetables, sweet and coffee can be had at the bar for about 13s. 6d., which is reasonable by U.S. train catering standards. It is staffed by two chefs, two waiters and a steward.

If you want to reserve sleeping accommodation on a train like the 'Empire Builder', there are facilities to suit the size of your wallet. In a European sleeping car, the accommodation is usually a standardized first or second class, but many U.S. cars offer a variety of berths within one coach body. The standard vehicle built for many railroads by the Pullman Standard company, for example, has six each of the cheapest open berths and of 'roomettes', with four of the more expensive bedrooms in the centre. In each type of accommodation the facilities are convertible, so that the passenger can use the berth comfortably for both day and night travel. The Americans pioneered the 'duplex roomette', an ingenious space-saving arrangement which dovetails overlapping compartments on two levels and thereby fits more of them into one car body without sacrifice of roominess; this layout is now employed in the latest European sleepers of the International Sleeping Car Co. The zenith of luxury on some U.S. transcontinental trains is the 'master suite', whose appointments rival those of a first-class hotel on *terra firma*.

There are five sleepers on the 'Empire Builder', each offering berths of different size and price. Marshalled in the middle of them are the train's dining car and the 'Great Dome' – the most striking car of the whole train. This is a massive 12-wheeler weighing 82 tons and standing 15½ft from rail level to roof, which is glazed from end to end to provide a 74-seater solarium extending the whole length of the car. The 'Great Dome' is built throughout on two storeys. Underneath the dome, which is reached by stairways at each end of the car, is a palatial 35-seater lounge-bar, with magazines on display and writing tables at which stationery headed with the train's name is available; an electrically-powered dumb waiter hoists drinks and snacks up from downstairs to passengers on the dome above. The 'Great Dome' carries its own 70-h.p. diesel-generator set to supply its electrical equipment and power its air-conditioning, which is a standard feature of U.S. expresses and for which power is normally taken from auxiliary engines on the diesel locomotives. The car is reserved for the use of 'Pullman' or first-class passengers.

Both the Milwaukee and Santa Fe operate similar 'Great Domes', which are built by the big U.S. coach-manufacturing firm of Budd. Other versions of the double-deck dome are also in use. The Union Pacific, for instance, runs some two-storey diners, with two dumb waiters to transport food from the kitchen to the upstairs dining saloon that is laid out beneath a glass-domed roof in the centre of the car; below the dome saloon is a charming private room with seats for 10 passengers.

To return to the 'Empire Builder', the last car in its rake is a sleeper with a bow-ended observation saloon at the rear. Observation saloons are another characteristic of the long-distance U.S. express and another feature for which some striking designs have been evolved by several railroads. And there, with the 'Empire Builder's' public address system discoursing recorded music to its passengers – one of the more controversial services on a U.S. train like this; my preference is for the Japanese version, which place individual passengers' headphones at each seat – we finish our tour of a typical American transcontinental luxury train.

One of the reasons why British Railways have opted in general for more stereotyped long-distance passenger coaches, without the frills of restaurant cars *and* two separate kinds of buffet or bar on the same train, is the obvious one that they add considerably to operating costs because of the extra train weight per passenger that the locomotive must haul. A full air-conditioning system, for example, may add some 4 per cent to the train dead weight per passenger seats – and no less than 10 per cent to the first cost of each car so equipped, to quote a German calculation. Although increasing use of light steel alloys and aluminium has enabled the Americans to keep their orthodox coach weights down to an average of between 40 and 50 tons in recent years, despite the 'gimmicks', the decline in patronage and rises in other costs drove some railroads in the 1950s to seek new ways to make their operations more profitable.

One of the big U.S. coach manufacturers, the American Car & Foundry Co., acquired in 1949 an interest in the device a Spanish engineer had conceived before World War II and built a prototype train for testing in the inventor's own country. R.E.N.F.E., the Spanish national

Although the Talgo idea for reduction of train weight did not prove popular in the U.S.A., it has been successful in the country of its invention, Spain. Here is a diesel-powered Talgo train of the Spanish National Railways on the regular Irun-Madrid service at Miranda de Ebro.

[*P. Ransome-Wallis*

railways system, found the idea well suited to its curving, not always ideally maintained 5ft 6in gauge lines and has operated 'Talgo' units, as they are called, for some years. At present they are running between Madrid and the Franco–Spanish border town of Irun on a mountainous route that reaches a 4,460ft summit 60 miles from the Spanish capital, and between Madrid and Barcelona; in each case they furnish luxury, first class only service – fast by Spanish standards, although the 400 miles between Madrid and Irun take as much as 8 hours 15 minutes and the train rarely exceeds 60 m.p.h. – that commands a special supplementary fare.

The Talgo train is rather like a monstrous caterpillar, for the coaches consist of short units flexibly jointed together. In the original Spanish version, each coach consisted of five units 20ft 2in long apiece, but the latest ones have three $34\frac{1}{2}$ft units; the Spanish cars' floor was a mere 18in above rail level, but in later models it is 26 to 28in, still achieving a very low centre of gravity. The floor of the cars is, in fact, below the level of their wheel centres and nestling on the

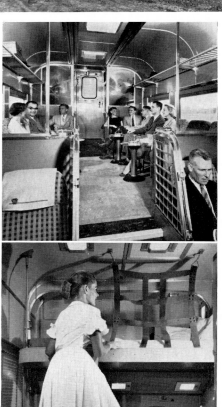

Above: One of the more successful U.S. experiments in lightweight coach construction was the New York-Washington 'Keystone' of the Pennsylvania Railroad, seen above with a Class 'GG-i' electric locomotive in charge. In the low-slung coaches, the normal underframe was dispensed with and underframe and body were combined in a tubular structure. Passengers sit in the depressed centre section of each car (*left*).
[*Pennsylvania Railroad*

Left: Typical convertible accommodation in the modern U.S. day and night train. For day use the upper berth folds back into the wall and the lower becomes a comfortable seat for both occupants of the compartment.

Above: Close-up of a Santa Fe 'Hi-Level' coach (*see page* 79). The low level is devoted to rest rooms, toilets and auxiliary equipment.

Below: This broadside view of a Baltimore & Ohio Railroad 'Slumberland' coach shows clearly the interlocking arrangement of 'duplex' berths. For a European version of this arrangement see page 78.

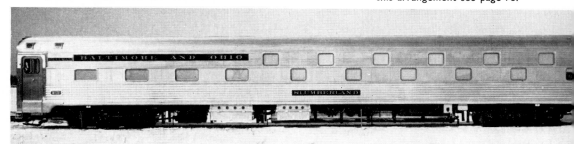

latter's stationary, 'U'-shaped axles. In the 3-unit car the centre unit is a 4-wheeler, but the other two each have an axle only at their outer ends; at their inner ends they ride piggyback fashion on the centre unit. The floors of the adjoining units overlap and are connected by a simple arrangement of pins; an acoustic blanket reduces noise within the car to the minimum and zip-fastened flexible diaphragms link the roofs and sides of adjacent units to make each 3-unit car fully enclosed. The special virtue claimed for the Talgo train is that its light weight and novel constructional methods, notably a secret system of mounting the single axles that steers and guides the wheels round curves, combine to permit higher speeds over sinuous routes in safety and comfort – and with less wear and tear on the track. Since each 3-unit car weighs no more than 30 tons but can be arranged to seat 84 passengers, there is also a good ratio of passengers to dead train weight.

The only 'vista-dome' observation cars running in Europe are the 'Panoramic' diesel railcars the French Railways have built to run in some of the more scenic territory of their system; however, the Germans may introduce non-powered vehicles of this kind before long on their 'Rheingold' service from the Hook of Holland via the Rhine Valley to Italy and Switzerland. Here is one of the French railcars, with two trailers attached, working from Marseilles to Le Mont-Dore via Nimes.
[M. Aubert

The Talgo principle was tried out in late 1955 by a U.S. railroad, the Rock Island, on a fast service between Chicago and Peoria and shortly afterwards by the New Haven between its namesake city and Boston; the latter was of special interest because the New Haven Talgo train was run throughout the $156\frac{3}{4}$ miles each way with a diesel locomotive at each end, to cut terminal turnround times. Also tested at this time was a startling rake of lightweight, air-suspended 4-wheelers built by General Motors and developed from this concern's standard road motor-coach body. The Pullman-Standard firm produced its own variant of the Talgo idea, again employing single-axle cars of lightweight aluminium alloy construction, which were introduced in complete trains on the New York Central and New Haven. Another system to experiment with ultra-lightweight trains of unconventional construction in the hope of cutting costs was the Pennsylvania, which produced a low-slung train of normal 85ft-length bogie cars, but employing

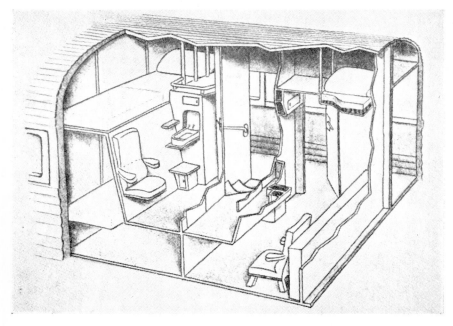

MODERN EUROPEAN SLEEPING CARS

A stainless steel car with interlocking berths of the International Sleeping Car Co. of Europe; this type of vehicle is now widely used on international night expresses. The drawing on the left shows the 'duplex' arrangement of berths.

The 86 ft 7 in length of the standard German Federal Railways coach of today is emphasized in the broadside view (below) of one of the latest sleeping cars operated by the German Federal Railway.

low-slung tubular bodies that dispensed with the normal underframes; named the 'Keystone', this was put on to the important New York–Washington service in 1956.

Not one of these ideas can be acclaimed a success that swept the nation – certainly not the single-axle cars; they have long since been taken out of service. The U.S. travelling public, for two decades accustomed to the lavish standards outlined in our description of the 'Empire Builder', soon showed their distaste for the more spartan accommodation and sometimes lively riding of the unorthodox cars; nor were they mollified by the prospect of cheaper fares if the latter became standard.

The German Federal Railway, incidentally, had no better luck with two Talgo-type light-weight trains of seven cars apiece, articulated on single-axle bogies, which it brought out in 1954; both have now been replaced by locomotive-hauled trains of conventional rolling stock. One was a day train for the Hamburg–Munich 'Blauer Enzian' service; and the other a remark-able outfit for the Hamburg–Zürich 'Komet', which had room for no more than 48 passengers, but offered them, in addition to a choice of sleeping berths or reclining seats, an all-night dining and bar service and a conference-room for industrious business executives.

The major railways of the world in general, therefore, have yet to be shown convincing proof that anything but a bogie car can produce that smoothness of ride and the spacious appointments that are among the chief selling points of rail travel *vis-à-vis* its modern competitors. That is not to say that there is no possibility of further reduction in manufacturing and operating costs by the use of different materials and methods in coach-construction. There is increasing recourse to lightweight metals and alloys; and in Britain a plastic coach body is a possibility. Plastics, which simplify cleaning and reduce maintenance costs because they can be produced in colour and never require repainting, are already employed widely in coach interiors.

Before we leave the U.S.A., we must look at a remarkable train which showed how more passengers could be carried in traditional U.S. luxury within the generous U.S. loading gauge – but at reduced cost. For its 'coach' class 'El Capitan' and Pullman class 'Super-Chief' expresses covering the 2,224 miles between Chicago and Los Angeles, the Santa Fe boldly ordered in the 1950s four trains built on two levels from end to end. Each one of these 85ft long 'Hi-Level' cars of Budd construction is 15½ft high from rail to ceiling. The principal passenger seating is all on the upper level, which is reached by winding staircases from the car's central entrance doors at ground level; the lower storeys are used for baggage compartments, crew quarters, rest-rooms, lavatories, the dining-car kitchen, and to house the trains' auxiliary power plant for electrical and air-conditioning plant. The *average* weight of these bulky cars is 67 tons – and the twelve-wheeled diners weigh considerably more; but even so they represent a sound economy in dead weight, for some of them combine the functions of two cars of conventional stock. In pre-'Hi-Level' days, the 14-car 'Super-Chief' weighed 835 tons, but had room for only 350 passengers; a 12-car train of 'Hi-Level' cars totals slightly less, at 803 tons, but can take 496 passengers.

In the first few years after the last war, the railways of Western Europe showed no inclination – nor could they see much need – to devise special luxury stock for front-rank express services, or to single out any for spectacular acceleration. In general, they were too concerned to repair the devastation of their systems and to restore a good average standard speed and comfort. But by the early 1950s it was obvious that in Europe, too, new concepts of train travel were needed to resist the challenge of road and air for the regular long-distance traveller, especially the businessman. One important result was the collaboration of six major Western European rail-ways to establish a Continental network of inter-city services, conforming to a common high standard of comfort and speed, and carefully scheduled at times convenient for the businessman to execute business at his destination and return home the same day.

Introduced in the summer of 1957, this 'Trans-Europe-Express', or 'T.E.E.' scheme, now embraces 17 different services that link nearly 100 important centres of commerce ranging from the Channel coast to Milan, Zürich, Munich and Hamburg. The trains were deliberately devised as self-contained units, to avoid time-wasting engine-changing and remarshalling at intermediate stops. They are first class only and all command a supplementary fare. Amongst the specifications agreed between the participating railway systems was that every 'T.E.E.' train should be fully soundproofed and that there must be arrangements to carry out Customs

79

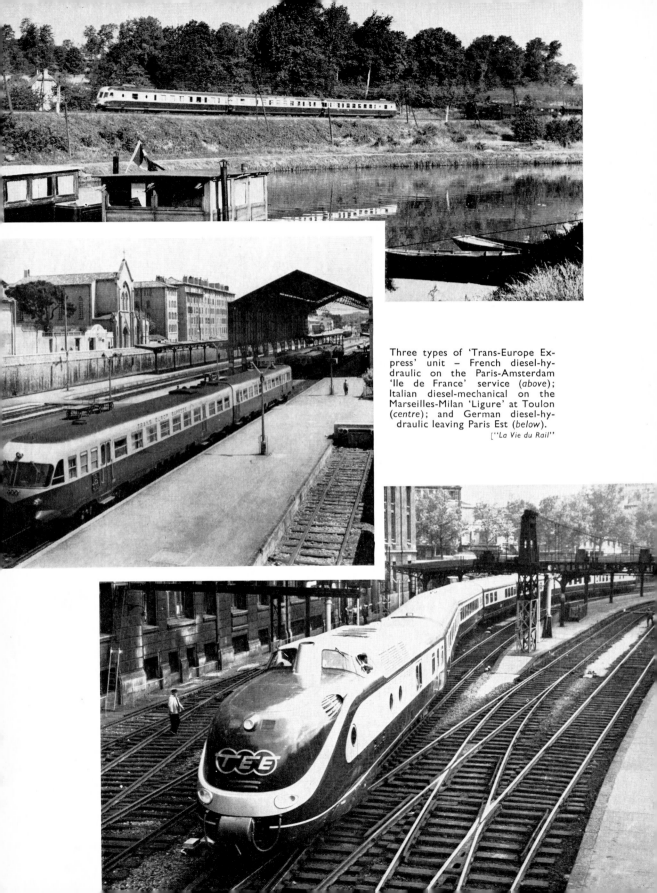

Three types of 'Trans-Europe Express' unit – French diesel-hydraulic on the Paris-Amsterdam 'Ile de France' service (*above*); Italian diesel-mechanical on the Marseilles-Milan 'Ligure' at Toulon (*centre*); and German diesel-hydraulic leaving Paris Est (*below*).

["*La Vie du Rail*"

Above: British motive power in South America—an English Electric 1,000 h.p. diesel-electric mixed traffic locomotive on the General Belgrano Railway, Argentina

[Blocks courtesy of English Electric Co.

Below: The 'Westlander' express of the Queensland Government Railways, hauled by an English Electric 1,500 h.p. diesel-electric locomotive

[Blocks courtesy of English Electric Co.

A British-built electric multiple-unit on the Rio suburban lines of the Central Railway of Brazil

[Blocks courtesy of Locomotive & Allied Manufacturers

examinations while passengers were on the move, to cut out tedious frontier stops. Another important feature of the scheme was the establishment of an international teleprinter system to facilitate seat reservation at the time of ticket booking by the passenger, no matter in which country he made his application; in addition, there were to be facilities for travellers to reserve seats in some ordinary express trains connecting with the 'T.E.E.' services.

There were some who wanted a fuller degree of standardization than has actually been achieved in 'T.E.E.' operation – for example, a comprehensive fare that would cover meals; and an international 'T.E.E.' staff that would relieve the passenger of all travel cares as soon as he entered railway property and even see his luggage through Customs examination. To the outside observer, the absence of conformity is most apparent in the luxury multiple-unit trains that four of the member railways contributed to maintain the 'T.E.E.' service – apart, that is,

'TRANS-EUROPE EXPRESS' UNITS

The latest of the 'Trans-Europe Express' units are these five-coach sets of the Swiss Federal Railways, the first in the T.E.E. scheme to work on straight electric power. The second vehicle of the unit is the 95-ton power car, which is equipped to enable the set to work off the four different voltages, including a.c. and d.c., which it encounters in its journeys between Zurich and Milan, and Milan and Paris.

from their standard 'T.E.E.' livery of red and cream. All the 'T.E.E.' trains, except for the latest Swiss products, are diesel-powered. This was inevitable at the time the scheme was inaugurated if the units were to run freely across frontiers; it is only in more recent years that developments in multi-voltage electric traction equipment have made electric operation possible.

The least ambitious are the 2- and 3-car French units providing the Paris–Zürich 'Arbalète', Paris–Amsterdam 'Ile de France' and Paris–Dortmund 'Paris-Ruhr'. Basically, these are diesel-hydraulic multiple-units of the same kind as the French National Railways employ for some of their own internal express services, with some refinements. The Italian units, used on the Geneva–Milan 'Lemano', Lyons–Milan 'Mont-Cenis' and Munich–Milan 'Mediolanum', are 2-car diesel-mechanical units built by Breda. To produce 90 passenger seats of 'T.E.E.' comfort standards in no more than two coaches *and* fit in the same unit a kitchen, train staff-room and office both for radio announcements to the passengers and for radio-telephonic calls by passengers to subscribers on *terra firma*, the Italians had to be unconventional. Each coach of the unit is 92ft 2½in long – nearly half as long again as a standard British Railways coach and the longest vehicles ever to run on the standard 4ft 8½in gauge in Europe.

The Swiss Federal and Netherlands Railways collaborated at the inception of the 'T.E.E.' scheme to produce five 4-car diesel-electric units which were built in Switzerland, with Swiss electrical equipment, but with Dutch diesel engines. These are a very different conception from the French and Italian sets, in which the power cars have room for substantial passenger accommodation. The power plant of each Dutch–Swiss unit is mounted in what is virtually a beefy 113-ton, 2,000-h.p. locomotive, except that just under a third of its body is left to house a luggage compartment and a room for Customs staff; the trailer at the other end has a driving cab in its streamlined nose for running in the reverse direction. Whereas French and Italian passengers take their meals at their seats in open saloons the Dutch–Swiss units have a separate restaurant car section, mix compartments and saloon accommodation – and offer every passenger adjustable reclining seats; moreover, their cars are fully air-conditioned and soundproofed, with double glass windows and draught- and dust-free inter-car gangways that have been completely enclosed like a hotel corridor by ingenious interlocking walls. How much more expensive the Dutch–Swiss units may be to operate than their companions is another matter; whereas an 825-h.p. French twin-set seating 81 tares 83 tons, a 2,000-h.p. Dutch–Swiss 4-car set (which also needs a 350-h.p. auxiliary engine for lighting, heating and air-conditioning supplies) accommodating 114, weighs 224 tons – practically two tons of train per passenger, which is a very high ratio for a multiple-unit. These Dutch–Swiss units are responsible for the Amsterdam–Zürich 'Edelweiss', Amsterdam–Paris 'Etoile du Nord' and Paris–Brussels 'Oiseau Bleu'.

As described in Chapter III, the Swiss introduced at the end of June, 1961 the 'T.E.E.' scheme's first electric multiple-units, capable of working off four different voltages. The technological development that made this possible was particularly welcome in view of the stiff gradients the Swiss trains would have to negotiate on the Gotthard and Simplon routes through the Alps in the course of their respective Milan–Zürich and Milan–Paris itineraries. The complex electrical equipment to enable each set to work off four different electrical systems is concentrated in a weighty 95-ton, 12-wheeled power car with four pantographs, one for each current encountered on the Paris–Milan journey, that is one of the inner vehicles in each of the four 5-car train sets; four of the six axles on the power car are motored to produce a total of 3,400 h.p. for only 257 tons total weight of train. Despite the intricacy of the electrical equipment, which no doubt is an important factor in the £330,000 price-tag of each unit, there is room in the power car for the kitchen, staff quarters and Customs examination-room; moreover, the driver's control gear is extraordinarily simple – he has only to switch up the correct pantograph and the electrical equipment automatically rearranges itself to suit the voltage the train is taking. Each unit has space for 126 passengers, all in open saloons, and meals are served in a separate restaurant-bar car. These are also the first 'T.E.E.' units to be arranged for a maximum of 100 m.p.h.; they provide the 'Gottardo' and 'Ticino' services between Zürich and Milan, and the very fast 'Cisalpin' between Milan and Paris, covering the 511 miles in 8 hours and averaging 80 m.p.h. throughout the 195·3 miles between Dijon and Paris.

The German units, which furnish the Hamburg–Zürich 'Helvetia', Ostend–Cologne–Frankfurt 'Saphir' and Paris–Hamburg 'Parsifal', are the flashiest in appearance and the most luxurious within the 'T.E.E.' fleet. Here again, the power is packed in what are all but locomotives – two bulbous-nosed 1,100-h.p. diesel-hydraulic units, one at each end of the 7-car set, which carry no passengers but only luggage and train or Customs staff. The German 'T.E.E.' units also are fully air-conditioned and soundproofed, but lightweight construction methods making considerable play with aluminium have kept the weight of each passenger car down to about 23 tons. The interior appointments are both appealing and comfortable; here again there is a choice of saloon or compartment accommodation, and not only a separate restaurant but also a cosy bar, while a frill that particularly appeals to me is the electro-pneumatic doors at the vestibule end of each car which fly open at a touch and then close automatically behind you.

Chapter III told of the world record with an electric multiple-unit which the Italians still hold. Since the war the Italian State Railways have pursued a policy of special, high-speed supplementary fare expresses with multiple-units which run to some of the fastest schedules in Europe –

A conspicuous characteristic of the latest Italian State Railways luxury electric multiple-units, like the seven-car 'ETR 300' type used on the Rome-Milan 'Settebello' and the four-car 'ETR 250' type (*right*), is the provision of an observation saloon in the rounded nose and the raising of the driving cab in a cockpit above it. The interior of the observation saloon is seen in the two illustrations (*below*); on the ETR 250 type it includes a refreshment bar.

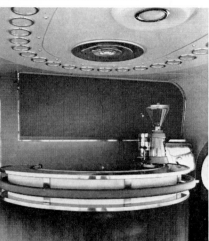

LUXURY ITALIAN ELECTRIC TRAINS

Below: Two interior views of what is perhaps the most luxurious train in Europe, the Rome–Milan 'Settebello' of the Italian State Railways. On the left is the refreshment car, with the restaurant visible beyond the bar; on the right is one of the 10-seater compartments, with fixed settees and individual armchairs, concealed luggage lockers behind the engraved panelling above the settee and a curtained Plexiglass wall separating the compartment from the corridor. The whole train is fully air-conditioned.

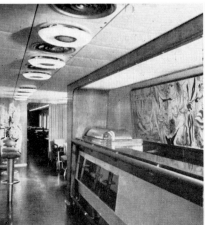

Above: The newest of the 3 ft 6 in gauge Japanese National Railways luxury expresses is the diesel-hydraulic 'Hatsukari', running the 469½ miles between Tokyo and Aomori. No fewer than eight of its nine cars are powered, with 14 180 h.p. engines spread throughout the train.

DE LUXE IN JAPAN

Left: This, believe it or not, is a narrow gauge train – the 'Kodama' between Tokyo and Osaka; notice the individual revolving armchairs and the portable telephone which can be fixed into various points in the car so that passengers can communicate with their friends on the ground. The ordinary first class accommodation, with reclining seats, is also seen (*above*).

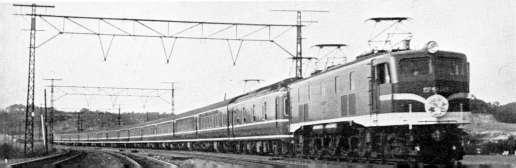

Left: The 'Sakura', a 14-car night train running from Tokyo to Nagasaki; the vehicle with pantographs next to the locomotive is a combined baggage and auxiliary power car.

a remarkable achievement to anyone who saw the ravaged Italian railway system immediately after the last war. The Italian speed palm currently goes to the 'Freccia del Vesuvio', which in the southbound direction covers the beautifully aligned and expensively constructed coastal race-track of 130½ miles from Rome to Naples Mergellina in 105 minutes, at a start to stop average speed of 74·6 m.p.h.

The most luxurious of the Italian multiple-units – and ones without superior in Europe – are the 7-car Type ETR 300 sets employed on the 'Settebello' between Rome and Milan. This, too, in relation to the fiercely sinuous route it follows between Rome and Florence and the long climbs beyond to the 1,058-ft summit near the Apennine Tunnel, is remarkable swift. Inclusive of intermediate stops at Bologna and Florence, each lasting five minutes, the southbound 'Settebello' is timed over the 393½ miles from Milan to Rome in 6 hours flat, so that it is required to average 67·5 m.p.h. all the time it is on the move over this largely difficult main line; across the flat Po Valley north of Bologna the 'Settebello' can be given free rein and its 12 bogie-mounted traction motors, with a total output of 3,040 h.p. for 364 tons of train, often get their chance to whip the unit up to its 100 m.p.h. maximum in maintaining a 74·9 m.p.h. booking for the 136 miles from Milan to Bologna.

When I rode the 'Settebello' over this stretch I was able to see the speedometer needle cross the three-figure mark in the driver's eyrie – cab is hardly the word for the airliner-like cockpit protruding its cupola through the roof of the end cars. It has been designed thus to leave the streamlined coach end free for a passengers' observation saloon; here you can sit right over the buffers, watching the route unfold before you and the track fly beneath your feet – the most thrilling vantage point for a train ride I have ever come across. The idea has now been re-produced in new 4-car Italian electric multiple-units of Type ETR250, which have been intro-duced on other services between Milan, Rome and Naples and between Milan and Venice.

The 'Settebello's' first-class-only passenger accommodation is entirely in 10-seater rooms; again, the traditional term 'compartment' scarcely seems suited to these beautifully styled lounges, with 3-seater sofas at each end, four loose armchairs and curtained plexi-glass walls on the corridor side of the car. The train is, naturally, fully air-conditioned and soundproofed and includes a buffet as well as a high-class restaurant. It is one of the growing number of European express services offering radio-telephonic communication with any subscriber on the national network.

An Asian country is now challenging the West for supremacy in rail-travel style and luxury – moreover, it is making its bid, not on 4ft 8½in, but on 3ft 6in gauge, which makes the capacious-ness of its streamlined fliers and the variety of their facilities the more remarkable. With their spread of electrification, the extent of which has been almost doubled since the last war and which has been justified by the great weight of traffic carried, the Japanese National Railways have developed the use of multiple-units for long-distance traffic. On the country's busiest main line, from Tokyo to Osaka, the J.N.R. are running in the middle of one of the globe's most intensive express service four beautifully-finished 12-car trains, strikingly liveried in red and yellow, which provide the twice-daily 'Kodama' and twice-daily 'Tsubame' services between the two cities. Each train makes an out-and-home trip of 690 miles daily; the timing for each leg is 6½ hours for the 345 miles, inclusive of stops, while in July, 1939, one of these trains was tested at up to 101 m.p.h. – a world speed record for narrow-gauge railways.

Like most modern high-speed trains, the J.N.R. streamliners are of lightweight construction, so that all 12 cars with their 1,500 volt d.c. electrical equipment total no more than 412¾ tons; and for that tonnage they can carry 598 passengers in great comfort – a ratio of train weight to passenger capacity that contrasts strongly, for example, with the Dutch-Swiss 'T.E.E.' units. Half of the cars are motored, with two traction motors on each bogie to produce a total output of 3,200 h.p. These fully air-conditioned trains abound in 'gimmicks'. Most of the first-class accommodation is in open saloons, with every seat both adjustable to a low reclining position and rotatable; each passenger has his own earphone through which he can listen to the national radio programmes, picked up by antennae on the car roof, and in a corner of the car is a neat writing-room. There is also a first-class parlour car, with individual, revolving armchairs, by each of which there is a plug into which the train staff can fix telephones for passengers to com-municate with their friends or businesses in Tokyo, Nagoya or Osaka; a kiosk at one end retails

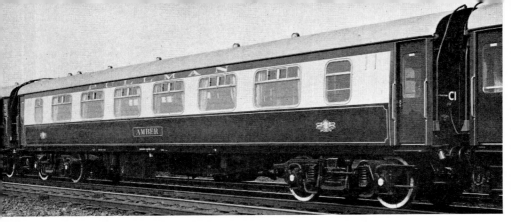

BRITISH RAILWAYS' NEW PULLMANS

(see facing page)

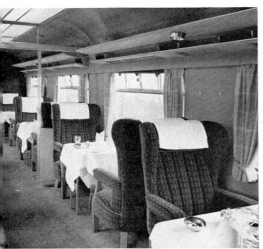

refreshments and magazines. In the buffet car there is a speedometer to show travellers the pace they are making; this car also includes a public telephone kiosk. Another novel device is an electrically-operated, illuminated indicator, suspended above the tables in the dining car, which keeps passengers informed of the position of the train on its route at any moment. The second-class cars, though less lavish than the first, are extremely comfortably open saloon vehicles. In 1960 the Japanese introduced similar 9-car trains, but diesel-powered with no fewer than fourteen 180-h.p. engines (only one of the nine cars is a trailer) and hydraulic transmission, on the 469½-mile 'Hatsukari' service over the non-electrified route between Tokyo and Aomori, in the north of Honshu.

No less striking are the three locomotive-hauled, 14-car night trains in deep blue livery, lined in cream, which the J.N.R. run south from Tokyo the length of the Honshu mainland, then underwater in the Kanmon Tunnel to destinations on Kyushu island – the 'Asakaze' to Hakata (749 miles), the 'Sakura' to Nagasaki (850 miles) and the 'Hayabusa' to Nishi-Kagoshima (942 miles). The variety and modernity of their 'roomettes' and sleeping berths are on a par with a North American transcontinental express. The end car of the 'Sakura' train set looks at first like an additional locomotive, for pantographs protrude from its roof; but in fact this is a combined baggage and auxiliary power car, picking up current from the overhead 1,500-volt d.c. traction supply to power generators feeding the train's heating, lighting, cooking and air-conditioning plant. On the Swiss Federal Railways, restaurant cars are similarly equipped so that their kitchens can work from the overhead current.

Notice that, with the exception of the American expresses and the Japanese night trains just described, all the services of which we have been talking are provided by self-contained multiple-units, formed into sets capable of coupling with each other and with driving cabs at each end of the train. This arrangement has decided advantages with some of the services involved. If the route involves reversals, as at Cologne in the case of some 'T.E.E.' trains or Florence with the 'Settebello', there is no engine-changing and the duration of the stop can be tailored to the time it takes the motormen to move from one cab to the other cab; thus the 'Saphir' takes only three minutes over its halt at Cologne. In the earlier days of the 'T.E.E.' service, the 'Saphir' and 'Rhein-Main' ran coupled together between Frankfurt and Cologne and because they had multiple-unit control connections one crew sufficed to drive both trains over this section. There was a further economy, since a train path over this busy section of main line was saved. The saving of crews and train-paths by manoeuvres of that kind is a great virtue of using multiple-units and the German Federal Railways timetable shows several instances of it with the 3- and 4-car units it employs on many of its own internal inter-city express services.

Despite this – and the fact that they were pre-pioneers in fast diesel multiple-units, as we saw in Chapter II – the Germans are now turning against express multiple-units in their future construction. If journeys do not include reversals, or if the terminal turnrounds between them are not short, there is less point in employing multiple-units. On some routes the demand for accommodation varies according to the time of day or season of the year; certain of the day's workings, for instance, may need lavish restaurant seating, while on others the custom is enough only to justify a buffet, and yet again some trains may want extra room for mail and parcels. The inability to vary the make-up of a multiple-unit makes it unsuitable for such services.

Travellers in particular hold it against multiple-units that no railway in the world seems able to produce one to ride as well as the best locomotive-hauled coaches. There is an inherent problem in achieving the same stability in trains which are being part-pulled and part-pushed by motors spread throughout them, front to rear, as in those hauled at the front by locomotives. There are some expensive alternatives. One is seen on the Japanese 9-car diesel multiple-unit mentioned above, which has engines on every car but one, to spread the power impulses as evenly as possible; but so many low-powered, high-speed engines must be a great deal more expensive to maintain than, say, the two 1,100-h.p. engines of a German 'T.E.E.' unit. Another possibility, with diesel-electric or straight electric traction, is to employ flexible drives from traction motors to driving axles, instead of hanging the motor partly on the axle and connecting the two by direct gearing; but not every railway engineer is agreed that fully-sprung traction motors make for better riding than those that are less expensively axle-hung.

In their 'T.E.E.' units the Germans have produced the smoothest-riding multiple-units I have sampled in Western Europe – and which gave me a considerably better ride than many I have had in good locomotive-hauled stock elsewhere. But even they do not equal the Germans' modern 86½ft locomotive-hauled coaches in this respect; these have no European equal, in my view. In the achievement of a high standard of riding, the German vehicles have the advantage of a length unsurpassed in Europe. Compare it with the British Railways standard of 64ft 6in, which we are powerless to increase without almost system-wide enlargement of clearances in stations, yards, bridges and tunnels, as otherwise the much longer frames would foul lineside structures when they swung round curves.

See how the credits and debits of the multiple-unit principle balance up in British Railways' diesel-electric Pullmans, which are our counterpart of the Continental 'T.E.E.' service. First let it be said that the 'Midland', 'Birmingham', 'South Wales' and 'Bristol Pullmans' set entirely new standards of British rail travel luxury and run to several '60 m.p.h.-plus' timings that call often on their 90-m.p.h. maximum speed; they can compete with the Continent's best in the luxury and style of their interiors, their comfort and the service they offer the passenger. The Pullmans are diesel-electric, with a 1,000-h.p. German-built M.A.N. high-speed engine in each end car and eight fully-sprung traction motors distributed among four of each unit's coaches, two to a bogie; in addition, a Rolls-Royce 190-h.p. diesel engine-generator set on each unit looks after the wants of its air-conditioning equipment and other electrical apparatus. The two 'Midland Pullman' units have six cars and are exclusively first class, but the three 8-car Western Region sets providing the Bristol, South Wales and Birmingham services include second-class saloons. The two kitchens in each unit serve meals at all seats, which are adjustable, reclining armchairs in the first-class cars. The Pullmans are the first fully air-conditioned and soundproofed trains to run in this country, with many a sales attraction, such as adjustable Venetian blinds between the double-glazed windows and enclosed, firm-floored inter-car gangways after the fashion of the Dutch–Swiss 'T.E.E.' units.

But should the trains have been multiple-units? On the Western Region, certainly, all three 8-car sets are now in service each week-day and have some fairly tight terminal turnrounds which make their multiple-unit characteristics an advantage. The 'Birmingham Pullman' has only 35 minutes in London between its morning run up from Wolverhampton and the return, and 55 minutes at Birmingham at midday before it sets out again for Paddington. Similarly, the 'Bristol Pullman' spends only half an hour at Bristol after its early afternoon run down from London, before its second sortie later in the day. But it was only in the 1961–2 winter that the third set was brought into daily use instead of being kept spare. At the time of writing, it is unfair to criticize the long period of idleness the 'Midland Pullman' fritters away in London between its morning run up from Manchester and evening return from St. Pancras, as a midday trip to Nottingham and back is temporarily suspended because of trades union objections. But, whether this is operating or not, the other spare set is idle every day – and with it 2,000 h.p. of expensive diesel-electric motive power, which cannot be detached for other jobs. Exactly the same waste is unavoidable with the spare 'Settebello' unit of the Italian State Railways.

The alternative is demonstrated on the Eastern Region, whose Sheffield Pullman service is a twice-daily, each-way luxury working mainly for businessmen running to fast schedules between London and the Yorkshire steel city. But this, like the other East Coast Route Pullman trains of British Railways, has been re-equipped, not with multiple-units, but with palatial new loco-motive-hauled cars. Undeniably they give the passengers a smoother ride than the multiple-units, but how much the difference is attributable to the method of propulsion and how much to other factors is debatable. What is a matter of fact is that the train is easily broken up to remove a single defective car and substitute a spare, whereas the profusion of control circuit and power cables, not to mention the enclosed gangways, on the diesel sets make it impracticable in their case; thus, considerably fewer than a full train of spare cars need to be maintained as a safeguard for the Sheffield service. But more important, while the Sheffield Pullman cars are idle each night, the expensive diesel power is available for other work.

U.S. passenger diesels in multiple-unit formation—four General Motors
2,000 h.p. diesel-electric units, the two outer ones with cabs and the two
inner ones cabless 'boosters', head the 'City of Portland' express of the
Union Pacific Railroad

[*Union Pacific Colourphoto*

The modern style in U.S. diesel traction—the mixed traffic 'hood unit'. There are three General Motors 2,000 h.p. Type GP-20 diesel-electric locomotives hauling Chicago–Kansas City freight for the Santa Fe Railway

[General Motors]

The high-speed electric 'Settebello', the luxury Rome–Milan express of the Italian State Railways, in the Apennine mountains between Florence and Bologna

[From a painting by V. K. Welsh

The 'Blue Train' of the South African Railways runs twice a week each way in summer and once a week in winter between Cape Town and Johannesburg, a distance of 956 miles, during which it climbs from sea level to 5,735 ft. The photograph shows a British-built electric locomotive of North British Loco. Co./G.E.C. construction hauling the southbound train out of Johannesburg

[Blocks courtesy of J. Stone & Co. (Deptford) Ltd.

V

RUNNING A MODERN RAILWAY

IN most of Western Europe the railways' chief competitor for passengers is the private car. Its attraction to the car-owner is its flexibility and convenience; at any time of the day that best suits him, the motorist can decide to set off on his journey without having to consult a timetable. However, with the modern forms of traction the railway operator is encouraged to compete with the private car on this very advantage it may seem to have made its own.

We have already remarked that the new forms of traction are decidedly more expensive than steam. Moreover, their expectation of life is shorter, for a main-line diesel locomotive is likely to be worn out within 15 to 20 years, whereas at the time of writing 30-year-old Gresley Class 'A3' Pacifics are turning in better performance and longer mileage between overhauls on top class main-line work than they have ever done. If the heavy cost of the new traction is to be recouped, therefore, its capacity for intensive work and its ability to cut journey times must be fully exploited.

This is an inducement to the operator to run more trains in his service, particularly since his operating costs per train-mile are invariably reduced with diesel and electric traction, compared with the days of steam. For example, when, at the beginning of 1961, the North Eastern Region of British Railways revitalized its Leeds–Huddersfield–Manchester service with new 'Trans-Pennine' diesel multiple-units on a through Hull–Liverpool run, by handing over the Liverpool–Newcastle expresses to Type '4' diesel-electric locomotives, and by improving the local feeder services to these trains, it increased its train mileage over the routes involved by close on 30 per cent; but, thanks to the employment of diesel traction, it was able to cut its operating expenses by 37 per cent, through such means as better utilization of rolling stock and economy in train crews (largely because only one engine-crew man was required on the diesel multiple-units).

If it pays to run more trains and they can be relied upon, with the new traction, to run with clockwork efficiency, the logical corollary is a timetable based on regular interval principles. If railway staff know that trains to X always leave Y at 30 minutes past each hour, the timetable becomes an instinct with them and punctuality usually improves. In much the same way, the timetable is soon impressed on the passenger's memory; providing it offers frequency as well as regularity of service, he rarely if ever needs to thumb over the timetable pages because it is always at the back of his mind that at a certain time in each hour he can be sure of a train from his local station. The trains become almost as convenient and easy to use as his own car.

The Southern Region of British Railways has built up its d.c., third-rail electrified services on just these principles. On the Sussex and Kent Coast main lines from London and their feeder branches the electric multiple-unit timetables operate to a regularly recurring pattern throughout the day, except for variations in the morning and evening peaks to allow the running of extra business trains. To the man of Kent regularly travelling to and from London, the sequence of his train service is now as ingrained as his mealtimes. It has become an instinct that at 40 minutes past each daytime, off-peak hour a 12-car Kent Coast multiple-unit express departs from London's Victoria station; that at Gillingham it will separate into two 4-car units for the coast line to Ramsgate, and one 4-car unit to Dover Priory; that for shorter-distance travellers there is always, just behind the express, a stopping train from Charing Cross, which will follow it from Gillingham and call at the intermediate stations the fast train misses; that at Sittingbourne a train from the Sheerness branch connects with the express; and that at Faversham the slow train from Charing Cross will overtake and exchange passengers with a preceding stopping train from Sheerness to Dover Priory. In reverse, the timetable pattern is similar for trains from Kent to London.

With almost every new diesel multiple-unit service introduced by British Railways nowadays a regular-interval timetable of this kind is established. The attraction of the principle is obvious from the big increases in patronage some of these schemes have obtained compared with the last months of steam working – since 6-car 'Inter-City' units were put on the Glasgow–Edinburgh line, for example, over 40 per cent more passengers have been using the railway between these two Scottish cities; the story is the same between Crewe, Stoke and Derby, where the standard diesel multiple-units operate, and in the Hampshire area, where the Southern Region runs 3-car diesel-electric multiple-units. Many other instances of the popularity of these new timetables and the trains which provide them could be quoted.

Apart from the Southern Region, whose latter-day interval-timetable schemes are extensions of a long-established principle, it is the Great Eastern Line of the Eastern Region which is now adopting the idea on the largest scale in Britain. The Great Eastern initiated a long-term plan to mould the passenger timetable of its entire system on a regular-interval basis in January, 1959, when it recast its Liverpool Street–Ipswich–Norwich service on the basis of hourly departures throughout the day from 8.30 a.m. to 8.30 p.m.; at the same times the connecting diesel multiple-unit services on the cross-country branches feeding the Ipswich main line were retimed on a matching interval basis, so that the expresses would make a recurring pattern of useful connections at the intermediate stops. Then, in November, 1960, the Great Eastern took advantage of its completion of a.c. electrification on the North-East London suburban lines to Enfield, Chingford, Hertford East and Bishop's Stortford, and the delivery of Type 3 diesel locomotives in the 1,600–1,700 h.p. range for its Liverpool Street–Cambridge–King's Lynn expresses, to bring all these services into its regular-interval working. Now Cambridge has a daytime express train service with London almost as frequent as Norwich.

When they were devising the new Cambridge line timetable, the Great Eastern planners focused a considerable share of their attention on the cathedral city of Ely, which is the hub of several branches radiating into East Anglia. They timed each two-hourly Liverpool Street–Cambridge–King's Lynn express and its opposite number in the up direction so that the pair of them arrived at Ely almost simultaneously, and made these two events the centre of a pattern of branch-line activity. Before the main-line trains come in, diesel multiple-units follow each other into Ely from Newmarket, Norwich and Peterborough (the last-mentioned has connected during its journey with another multiple-unit, originating from Wisbech, at March); these locals feed passengers into the expresses, which in their turn put off some passengers for the branches; and so, when the expresses have gone their opposite ways, the diesel multiple-units set out again for their branches in reverse order – first a Wisbech train, this time connecting with a Peterborough service at March, then the Norwich unit and finally the Newmarket one.

By pivoting the northern end of their Cambridge main-line service on Ely, the Great Eastern's timetable architects combined convenience to their patrons with some worthwhile economic gains. Since the inter-connection of all these trains occurs within 45 minutes, the branch multiple-units can be turned round fairly quickly – and the use of diesel multiple-units facilitates this in a station that is not capacious – for their return journeys from Ely. Thus each branch gets its own good interval service, with the bonus of much better cross-country connections than it ever had before, at no extra cost in rolling stock, motive power or crew workings – indeed, there is a saving under these three headings, because the men and equipment are being intensively utilized for more work than was the case with the old steam timetable. But in case I have given the impression that Ely is the only focal point of this Great Eastern timetable, it must be emphasized that, as well as arranging operations neatly at this junction, the planners had also to time the stops of the London–Cambridge–King's Lynn trains each way at Bishop's Stortford so that they would connect there both with the North-East London electric multiple-unit service, which runs to its own interval pattern, and with a diesel multiple-unit service covering the intermediate stations between Bishop's Stortford and Cambridge. They had also to interweave the expresses with the intensive North-East London regular-interval electric suburban service on the restricted number of tracks at the approach to Liverpool Street Station, in London.

The Great Eastern expresses between London, Ipswich and Norwich, and between London, Cambridge and King's Lynn, are diesel locomotive-hauled. We have already observed in a previous chapter that a virtue of multiple-units is the simplicity with which their formations can be increased or reduced to meet traffic demands (though the type of accommodation they offer cannot be varied). It is not quite so simple to vary the formation of a locomotive-hauled train. First of all, more manoeuvring is involved, because a shunting locomotive usually has to be called up to remarshal the coaches and these operations are bound to block part of the station layout for a time. Second – and perhaps more important – the performance of the diesel locomotive is, as we have said before, absolutely predictable; this means that the railway operators know what it will *not* do, as well what they can be sure it will. If they have based their timings on the known ability of a diesel locomotive to haul nine coaches from X to Y in 30 minutes start to stop, it will inevitably need more time for the run if they try to attach two more coaches to its train; for there is no 'extra ounce' of energy to be won in an emergency from a diesel or electric locomotive, beyond its known best, as there usually is from a well-maintained steam locomotive if the fireman heroically steps up his firing to increase the boiler's steaming rate.

If, therefore, the railway operator wants to make the economic best of diesel and electric traction, he aims at a regular-interval timetable following as slavishly as possible a regular pattern of timing and loading. But if he has to use both multiple-units and locomotive-hauled trains to achieve his ends, as they do on the Great Eastern Line of the Eastern Region, he must try to run his locomotive-hauled expresses as much like multiple-units as possible. They must be of a standard formation of coaches, carefully arranged to satisfy as far as possible the traffic needs, say, of both a breakfast-time service to London which carries a large number of business-men, and a midday service to the country, on which more of the passengers are likely to be travelling for pleasure; if the trains do not have to be remarshalled between journeys the coaches can be turned round to form a return service as quickly as their locomotives. By following these principles, the Great Eastern Line is making more trains available to its customers than ever before, but each train is cheaper to operate because its locomotives and coaches are covering more miles every day. On the Liverpool Street–Ipswich–Norwich route, which is only 115 miles from end to end, nine train sets are enough to provide 13 workings each way and two of those formations complete two double journeys, totalling 460 miles, in a day. On the London–Cambridge–King's Lynn line, eight more trains incorporate a buffet car than was the case in the 1960 summer timetable, but the Great Eastern Line had to acquire only one more buffet car to effect this improvement in its rewritten timetable, because its previous stock of these vehicles is now utilized more intensively through the quicker turnrounds of staple train formations.

In days gone by British expresses carried many more through coaches, detached at stops *en route* to serve places whose traffic did not merit a full train to themselves, than they do nowadays. It is true that the Southern Region still runs a train as remarkable on this count as the 'Atlantic Coast Express', which is made up of 12 coaches in no fewer than nine different portions – two coaches for Ilfracombe, single coaches for Torrington, Padstow and Bude, two coaches for Plymouth, a restaurant-car set which goes no farther than Exeter and single coaches for Exmouth, Sidmouth and all stations from Salisbury to Honiton (this last goes forward from Salisbury attached to a stopping train) – but there is nothing like it on any other Region. The concept of a frequent, regular-interval main-line service does not encourage through coach working and the Great Eastern Line has had to cut out several operations of this kind.

Here again, it is practicable with multiple-units; in the North-East London electrified service of the Great Eastern, for example, an 8-car train sets out from Liverpool Street every half-hour and at Broxbourne is quickly divided in two, one 4-car set for Hertford, the other for Bishop's Stortford. Coming back to London, the two units are re-united as one train at Broxbourne. Each unit has its own power plant so that it can move off as it is parted from its twin. We have already quoted a longer-distance example of this kind of operation while discussing the Southern's Kent Coast service, wherein each express from and to Victoria is separated into and reassembled from Ramsgate and Dover Priory portions at Gillingham. With a locomotive-hauled service, on the other hand, when a through coach is separated from its main train it must be shunted on to another train to complete its journey; additionally, it may make difficult the maintenance of fixed train formations; and finally, a through coach service often requires the provision of special vehicles incorporating on one set of frames all the services needed – first- and second-class accommodation, guard's and luggage-room – which are not so useful on other services. However, the abandonment of some through coaches does not mean slower journeys; for example, although

Wisbech passengers on the fast Liverpool Street–Cambridge–King's Lynn 'Fenman' must now change into a multiple-unit at Ely, whereas before they had a through coach all the way, they get to Wisbech earlier than they did despite having to change trains, for the abolition of this and other through-coach workings has helped the authorities to accelerate the whole service.

The outstanding European example of a regular-interval timetable is offered by the Netherlands Railways. Steam was completely banished from this system by 1958. Just over one-half of the Dutch route mileage is electrified at 1,500 volts d.c. and employs chiefly multiple-units for passenger services, with electric locomotives for the long-distance international expresses running into and out of the Netherlands and for freight work. On the remainder of the system diesel-electric multiple-units monopolize the passenger workings and for freight traffic there are diesel-electric locomotives, which at night may also render assistance in the electrified areas, where the business is naturally the most brisk and the freight movements are the heaviest. In selecting their motive power the Netherlands Railways worked on the logical theory – which I have simplified somewhat for brevity – that, if their passenger traffic at all hours of the day was sufficient to justify X trains, but their peak-hour demands increased requirements to Y trains, they would need X multiple-units for their basic service, while the difference between X and Y would be covered by locomotive-hauled trains whose motive power could be used on other duties, principally freight, in the off-peak hours. Thus, at night, when the freight workings are at their zenith, extra locomotives are available; but these additional locomotives are not idle during the daytime, nor do the Netherlands Railways have to keep a large surplus of multiple-units chiefly to cope with the rush-hour, but to lie about at stabling points at other times of the day – as, I am afraid, do some Regions of British Railways.

Over 85 per cent of Dutch rail travel is short distance, of not more than 40 miles per passenger, and most of it is made on the electric multiple-units, which are operated to one of the strictest patterns in the world. It is even simpler to attach and detach these units than those of British Railways, for they are fitted with an all-purpose coupler that automatically connects braking, lighting and other control lines between sets, as well as coupling them together physically. The entire Dutch passenger timetable is built on an interval scheme so rigid that in general the station workings at the bigger centres are repetitive throughout the day in their allocation of the same platform to trains on specific routes, and to services which connect with each other. The same practice, incidentally, has been initiated by the Great Eastern Line of British Railways at Liverpool Street since its North-East London electrification; Enfield and Chingford trains now start from and arrive at Platforms 1–3 exclusively, the Bishop's Stortford and Hertford combined trains from Platform 4, the Lea Valley suburban trains from Platform 6 and the Cambridge expresses from Platform 7 – another benefit of patterned working to the passenger.

The Dutch have stepped farther and organized their night-time freight working as far as possible on the same lines, in order both to promise overnight delivery of merchandise, to keep the country's internal freight traffic clear of the lines busily occupied by frequent passenger trains during the day, and to utilize locomotives to the maximum. The railway system is divided for freight working into zones, each with its own marshalling yard, and between the yards there plies a nocturnal network of fast merchandise freight trains averaging 55 m.p.h. on the open main lines. The marshalling yard working is highly organized and standard timings are laid down for many of the regular activities, such as breaking up a feeder freight train from local goods stations and getting its wagons on to the right tracks for attachment to the trunk freight trains. These local feeder services roll into each yard between 7 and 9 p.m. every night; from 9 p.m. to midnight they are sorted and marshalled into the main-line services; and between midnight and 1 a.m. the main-line freights pull out on their runs to other yards, few of which will be more than three hours away, for the Netherlands is not a large country. The yards are now clear and their sorting sidings are reallocated to suit the sorting of the incoming trunk freights, which are received between 1 and 3 a.m.; by 5 a.m. the yards have dispersed the last of these to their sorting sidings and now the local goods trains set out in each zone, nearly all of them to reach their destinations before the tracks must be cleared for the morning rush-hour.

Neighbouring Belgium has not electrified so extensively as the Dutch, but on the important rail arteries which it has converted a similar train service pattern is operated. Over the 72-mile

MODERN RAILWAYS IN BELGIUM...

Up-to-date traction in modern surroundings – electric multiple-units of the Netherlands Railways in one of the system's impressive post-war stations, Utrecht.
[*Netherlands State Railways*

Left: A stainless steel electric multiple-unit of the Belgian Railways on the Luxembourg-Brussels service at Libramont.
[*B. Knowlman*

Right: A Belgian-built 1,750-h.p. diesel-electric locomotive with American power plant pauses at Namur on an express from Tournai to Liège.
[*B. Knowlman*

One of the four-car electric multiple-units which cover a large proportion of the Netherlands Railways' frequent, regular-interval passenger services.
[*Netherlands State Railways*

...AND THE NETHERLANDS

main line from Ostend to Brussels Midi, for example, there is a train each hour all day, running in most cases to a timing of 73 minutes – very nearly a mile a minute average, that is, despite intermediate stops at Bruges and Ghent. The Brussels–Ostend line is one of the best-aligned in Europe for high speed and in the summer of 1939 the Belgian Railways operated over it the fastest trains in Europe at that time – two steam-powered expresses daily in each direction which reeled off the journey in an even hour and averaged close on 75 m.p.h. between Brussels and Bruges. True, today's electric trains do not equal this standard; but herein lies an important principle of the regular-interval timetable; namely that you raise the *general* level of train speed to the highest possible common level, and do not single out one or two services for spectacular acceleration. To keep paths clear for extra-fast trains the operators must sacrifice track capacity and hence some frequency of service. If all trains run at the same speed there is room for a larger number at regularly-spaced intervals than if one is scheduled so fast that, on one side, it catches up and tries to 'bump' its more leisurely predecessor out of the timetable, while on the other it leaves behind it a wasteful 'vacuum' of track because its successor is travelling at much slower pace.

In the bigger European countries, however, a frequent day-long main-line service is not the rule. Take, for example, the now world-famous electrified 'race-track' of the French Railways from Paris to Dijon, and beyond to Italy, Switzerland, or to Lyons, Marseilles and the French Riviera – the route of the crack 'Mistral'. In the summer timetable current as I write there is no express departure from Paris to the south between the 9.15 a.m. and the 12.25 and 1.10 p.m. 'Mistral'; and after the 'Mistral' the timetable is bare of fast trains on this line until the start of the procession at 6.23 p.m., behind which stream the 7.25, 7.28, 7.53, 8.0, 8.10, 8.13, 9.2, 9.10, 9.13, 9.43, 9.50, 9.52, 10.15, 10.30, 11.0, 11.43, 11.46, 11.50 p.m., 12.5 and 12.8 a.m. The French are justly proud of the fact that scarcely one express traversing the 317·4 miles between Paris and Lyons is timed to average less than 60 m.p.h. between stops – many of them considerably more – and that every single one of the country's largest cities, as well as some beyond French borders, like Brussels and Basle, have at least one daily service with Paris averaging a mile-a-minute or better; but the French practice of grouping expresses at certain periods of the day and leaving slower traffic to make its own pace at other times undeniably facilitates the maintenance of such high levels of train speed.

Even over the shorter distance of 155·9 miles between Paris and the great northern industrial city of Lille, France's most recently a.c.-electrified main line, there are the same lengthy gaps in the timetable; after the 7.30, 8.0 and slower 9.36 a.m. from Paris the traveller from the capital has only the 11.45 a.m. to Lille until the 1.9 and 1.15 p.m.; there is a decidedly leisurely departure at 2.24 p.m., but then nothing until an evening flush of trains begins at 5.9 p.m. This is the service currently showing the world's fastest start-to-stop run in a booking of 29 minutes for the 41·1 miles from Arras to Longueau (average 84·9 m.p.h.) by the 11.45 a.m. from Lille. The 11.45 is one of the four crack businessmen's trains in each direction on this route, five of which are allowed only 130 minutes for the 155·9-mile run, inclusive of two stops *en route*; they are light-weight 5-coach, first-class-only trains of stainless steel stock with reclining seats, meals served at all seats, a bar for drinks and snacks and a radio-telephone callbox for communication with any subscriber on the French national telephone network.

The distance between two German cities that are a pair of Europe's biggest commercial centres, Hamburg and Cologne, is 286·3 miles; from King's Cross to Newcastle the mileage is 268·3 – very nearly as far. But whereas the German Federal Railway offers no through service from Cologne to Hamburg between 7.50 a.m. and 11 a.m., and trains at 12.39, 2.54 and 4.38 p.m. only until the early evening, King's Cross dispatches expresses to Newcastle each week-day at hourly intervals, with very slight variations, from 8 a.m. to 5 p.m. The tradition of a frequent daytime express service over distances of 200 miles-plus is stronger and more generally practised on British Railways than on any other world system of the same size, with the conspicuous exception of Japan. Even on a main line such as the Western Region's from Paddington to the West Country, which certainly carries an immense holiday-making traffic in the summer but for the rest has only Exeter and Plymouth – scarcely two of the country's principal commercial cities – to promote all-the-year-round travel on a substantial scale, it has been thought worth-while to put on an augmented, two-hourly interval express service in the autumn of 1961. Here again, the completion of new locomotive deliveries to make possible the dieselization of all express services on this route has been partially a spur to timetable revision.

All very well, observe some critics: these new and augmented services on an interval basis are admirable – but they are years too late. The stable door is being bolted with the horse, if not well away, at least half-way through the entrance; why could we not have had services of this kind long ago with steam, before the drift of traffic to the roads and the air became so substantial? Undoubtedly there was on British Railways plenty of scope for more imaginative redrafting of timetables than was carried out in the first decade after World War II; there was a tendency on too many lines to regard a pattern of principal express services which had existed since the 1930s as sacred and to be amended only in small details, not rewritten from first principles. Nevertheless, a fast, regular-interval service does demand the right tools for its perfect execution. Some of the difficulties encountered if the attempt is made without them are evident from an examination of another scheme of this kind initiated in the 1961–2 winter – the accelerated East Coast Route timetable, employing 22 English Electric 3,300-h.p. diesel locomotives.

[Continued on page 100

A MODERN B.R. DIESEL DEPOT

Compare the spaciousness and cleanliness of one of British Railways' new diesel maintenance depots with the cramped conditions and grime of the steam locomotive shed shown in the pictorial sequence illustrating steam locomotive servicing on pages 96–99. Both these depots are in North London. The diesel depot shown here is at Finsbury Park, on the Eastern Region, and services the diesel locomotives employed on the Great Northern Line's London area suburban and freight services, and those on East Coast route expresses. Two-level staging and inspection pits between the running rails allow the depot staff to work on their charges at three different levels. In the picture below are seen, from left to right, Brush Type '2' English Electric Type '1', Brush Type '2', and English Electric Type '2' diesel-electric locomotives.

[British Railways

A 'ROYAL SCOT' VISITS CAMDEN DEPOT, LONDON

The disposal of a 'Royal Scot' on shed

photographed by
H. G. FORSYTHE

The approach road from Euston station, London to Camden motive power depot, just visible at the extreme left in the view (*above*) of the north end of the running shed, brings 'Royal Scot' 4–6–0 No. 46126 *Royal Army Service Corps*, tender-first (*centre*), towards the turntable (*below*), which the locomotive operates itself through its vacuum brakepipe. After turning, the 4–6–0 moves to the next stage of servicing, following its arrival from Carlisle on the 'Northern Irishman'. In the picture above the engines

(continued opposite)

(continued from facing page) on view are, from left to right: 'Jubilee' 4-6-0 No. 45553 *Canada*, Class '5' 4-6-0 No. 44948, 'Royal Scot' No. 46148 *The Manchester Regiment* and 'Jubilee' 4-6-0 No. 45703 *Thunderer*.

No. 46126 has gone for coaling; the turntable is immediately returned by hand to the approach road ready to receive the next incoming locomotive (*above left*).

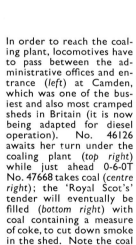

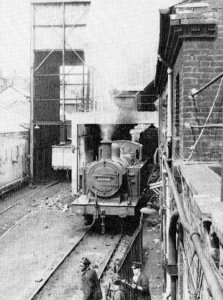

In order to reach the coaling plant, locomotives have to pass between the administrative offices and entrance (*left*) at Camden, which was one of the busiest and also most cramped sheds in Britain (it is now being adapted for diesel operation). No. 46126 awaits her turn under the coaling plant (*top right*) while just ahead 0-6-0T No. 47668 takes coal (*centre right*); the 'Royal Scot's' tender will eventually be filled (*bottom right*) with coal containing a measure of coke, to cut down smoke in the shed. Note the coal wagon on the left being hoisted to replenish the coal hoppers of the plant.

After the 'Royal Scot's' tender has been coaled, the tank is rapidly filled with water (*left*).

Royal Army Service Corps passes under the tower of Camden's modern ash plant (*left*) which unfortunately is temporarily out of order; thus ash disposal has to be carried out by hand (*right*). Shed staff appear to be fighting a losing battle with mountains of hot ash which normally would have been removed expeditiously in the ash plant's narrow-gauge trucks running in pits.

Over the ash pits, No. 46126 has her hopper ashpan doors opened before her fire is cleaned (*above right*); after fire-cleaning, the ashpan is raked (*above left*).

Smokebox cleaning (*left*) is the dirtiest job at the depot. No. 46126 stands over the ash-pits while accumulated soot and ash is raked and shovelled out. Left uncleared, it would block the lowest boiler tube outlets and impair the locomotive's steaming.

Photography by
H. G. FORSYTHE

A 'ROYAL SCOT' VISITS CAMDEN DEPOT, LONDON

(concluded)

Now cold, No. 46126 stands open for inspection and repair in the running shed (*centre right*); preparation for her next turn of duty includes lubrication (*bottom right*) by a fitter. Cleaning should be carried out during and after this stage, but just now Camden has only two instead of 32 cleaners, so No. 46126 will not be cleaned during this visit.

Finally, No. 46126 will be stabled in the running shed (*below*), where many other locomotives are already standing awaiting attention or a spell of duty. On the left, an English Electric Type '4' diesel-electric keeps company with another 'Royal Scot'; a rebuilt 'Patriot' class 4–6–0, No. 45536 *Private W. Wood, V.C.*, stands over the deep inspection pit in the middle road, with another 'Royal Scot', No. 46101 *Royal Scots Grey*, on the right.

The original British Railways Modernization Plan of 1955 envisaged 25,000 volts a.c. electrification of the East Coast main line from King's Cross to Doncaster and Leeds, and possibly from Doncaster to York as well. When it came to realities, however, the engineers found they could not cope simultaneously with the conversion of West Coast and East Coast Routes; and since then rising costs and the tricky financial situation of British Railways have made it unlikely that the already deferred East Coast electrification will be put in hand for several years to come, if at all. The Eastern and North Eastern Regions had therefore to adapt for implementation by diesel traction their schemes, originally conceived with electric traction in mind, to recapture the best express speed standards of 1939 – but with a very important difference: that whereas, in the years immediately before 1939, three streamlined fliers only were setting a pace to Newcastle, Edinburgh and Leeds greatly in advance of the general run of expresses, in the 1960s the aim should be for the pre-war streamliner timings to be the *average* of an interval express service to the North offering considerably more trains than before the war. At the southern end of the East Coast Route, in particular, the operators were convinced that the competition from road and air transport would never be met unless the 1955 Modernization Plan predictions of 75 m.p.h. average and 100 m.p.h. maximum speeds were fulfilled by as many of their expresses as possible.

To achieve these aims, the East Coast Route knew they would need a locomotive more powerful than the 2,000-h.p. English Electric Type '4' diesels which they were given to begin their main-line dieselization in the late 1950s, for these, reliable enough in themselves, were not designed to perform more spectacularly than a steam Pacific in good condition and well driven. The East Coast authorities made a case for diesels with at least 3,000 h.p. under the bonnet and were given the 'Deltics' – but only 22 of them, since they were very expensive pieces of machinery, costing about three or four times as much as electric locomotives of the same – or even higher – power. Now although each 'Deltic' could be utilized for 205,000 miles' running a year, better than twice the norm for a top-rank British steam express locomotive, this would not be enough to provide 'Deltic' haulage for every principal express. Electrification would have given the operators locomotives and multiple-units with almost identical acceleration and running characteristics, at least up to 60 m.p.h. or thereabouts; this would not only have made timetable planning easier, but also have increased the capacity of the line. For a year or two, certainly, the 'Deltics' would have to share the tracks with steam and other diesel locomotives whose characteristics did not match their own, and that would prevent realization of the kind of service originally contemplated. The reasons will become clear if we turn now to the modern methods of timetable compilation and train service organization.

With steam the planning of locomotive duties, generally speaking, has followed the detailed revision of a timetable. On British Railways it is the job of a diagramming office at each Regional headquarters, after they have been presented with the redrafted timetable, to piece the locomotive needs for each train into suitable daily duties, or diagrams, for the motive power of each depot in their Region that will, as far as possible, give each locomotive a respectable, revenue-earning daily mileage. Every effort is made to avoid 'unbalanced' working – that is, leaving a locomotive stranded far from its home shed without a suitable train to bring home, and therefore no option but to return, wastefully, light engine; and in most cases each diagram is of no more than 24 hours' duration, so that the locomotive regains its home depot for daily maintenance. On some lines, however, the development in recent years of the general-purpose locomotive concept has increased the employment of so-called 'cyclic' diagramming with steam power, giving them duties of several days' duration which may 'board' them out at strange sheds for a night or two. Engine-crew rosters must be devised separately, for, unlike his locomotive, an engineman's shift of work must not exceed eight hours; moreover, he must have learned the routes over which he drives. The planning of steam locomotive and crew workings is therefore a fascinating exercise in jigsaw work by diagramming and motive power administrations, ensuring that all trains are efficiently hauled by motive power suitable for their rostered loads and the routes involved; that each depot has adequate locomotives of the right classes to cover its diagrams and work which its crews are competent to perform; that the locomotive diagrams leave ample time for servicing; and that the crew diagrams do not risk work beyond the shift limit (to avoid this, locomotives may have to be remanned in the course of their journeys).

The main job of the Traffic Control offices of British Railways is the supervision of freight train operation. It is their task, not only to see that the goods trains run to time, but also that they are run economically. If loadings are light, they try to combine trains; if traffic is very heavy, they must see whether additional trains can be run, bearing in mind the urgency of the demand and the availability of engines, train crews and a train path in the timetable. This is the Eastern Region's District Control office at Doncaster. On the right is the desk of one of its Doncaster Section Controllers, each of whom is responsible for the traffic in one of the six sections into which the Doncaster District is divided for this purpose. The vital piece of the controller's equipment, which is built into his desk, is a telephone panel, through which he can speak to and be reached from every important operating point in his section – signalboxes, yards, stations, and shunter's cabins. Assisting the Section Controllers are Motive Power and Relief Controllers; the last-mentioned are responsible for the organisation of train crews to meet hour-to-hour traffic demands.

[British Railways

With diesel and electric traction, properly employed, however, diagramming and timetable planning go hand in hand. As we have already established, to recoup the massive capital expenditure on a diesel locomotive like the 'Deltic' it must be intensively utilized; to make a case for the purchase of 22 locomotives, the operators must be able to prove their ability to find each one revenue-earning work to the order of about 4,200 miles (the equivalent of 15 London–Newcastle runs) a week; and to arrange this, taking into account the requirements of the mechanical engineer for maintaining the locomotives at their base depots, it may be necessary to shape the timetable to suit the diagrams. One of the arts of modern timetabling is to achieve a compromise between the public demand for trains scheduled to their convenience, and the desirability to the railways of running trains at the times that effectively balance diagrams and make the most efficient use of locomotives, rolling stock and train crews.

In the preparation of diesel traction diagrams attention must be focused on the periodical maintenance of each unit. Each locomotive will probably be sent out from its depot on a cyclic diagram of five days' duration, during which it will pause between runs only for refuelling and a brief daily examination of its salient components. The concluding leg of the diagram must return it to its base depot for a period of maintenance on a carefully scheduled programme. Exemplary maintenance is vital if each locomotive is to perform to theoretical standards.

But the 'Deltic'-hauled trains, however important, are only a tiny proportion of the whole East Coast Route traffic. They must be interwoven with the remainder, passenger and freight, and the means of achieving this are best worked out graphically. The Trains Office of every British Railways Traffic headquarters keeps huge graphs for each route over which it has the timetabling responsibility. There is a graph for each section of line, marked off horizontally in time, and vertically by distance, with a note in the vertical margin of all the stations, yards, sidings and signal-boxes at which trains may stop for traffic purposes, or which are used as regular timing points (for trains passing non-stop, as well as those stopping) in the railwaymen's private working timetables. The railwaymen's working timetables, by the way, show every booked train working, passenger, parcels and freight, and a great deal more information that is not revealed in the public timesheets. The timing graphs are a maze of criss-crossing lines, each one representing

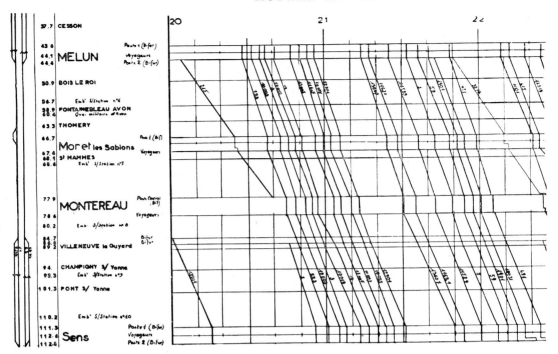

A small section of a timetabling graph for the Paris–Dijon main line of the French Railways. It covers the running for a peak holiday evening and demonstrates the high degree of track occupation possible with electric traction. The steep slope of the train lines illustrates the high average speeds, as a result of which a large number of trains can be pathed; notice also that the slope of most of the lines is identical, demonstrating the common standard of performance that can be expected with electric locomotives, so that the work of the timetable planners is simplified.

the path of a booked train. Assuming that the vertical marking of the distances is in the down direction from bottom to top, the lines on the graph leading in a north-easterly direction will be the paths of down trains, those crossing them in a south-easterly direction the paths of up trains. Where the graph line of a train is interrupted by a horizontal 'step', its progress is halted physically – but time goes on: in other words, the train has stopped *en route*. Obviously the lines on the graph that are nearest a horizontal pitch are those of the slowest trains, while those that are nearest the vertical represent the fastest; and where one of the latter lines converges with one of the former, a fast train has caught up a slower one, so that, unless the meeting takes place at a point where the slower train can be sidetracked to let the following one overtake, the fast train will get a signal check. These graphs, by the way, show trains' office staffs at a glance when and where they can fit in special trains.

If you take a piece of squared paper and mark it off in units of distance and time just as they do a railway timetable graph, then draw on it a series of parallel diagonal lines to represent trains, you will find you have room for more lines running all the way from top to bottom of the graph the nearer you draw them all to the vertical. Translating this into practical railway timetabling terms, it means that the faster the trains run, the more of them can each section of track accommodate – in other words, so much the more is line capacity increased. To make the exercise simple, you have drawn parallel lines; and that means that all the trains you have drawn in are running at the same speed. The nearest railways can come to that ideal is by adopting electric traction.

When you begin to raise the angle of the lines on your graph, the outermost will start to run off it before they reach the bottom; that means that the trains they represent cannot complete your imaginary section of track within the same period of time. Alternatively, raise the angle of only a few lines and you will get the same result, for ones you have not redrawn must be pushed back to prevent them bumping into the altered lines; on the track, the effect is that your fastest trains must be held back to prevent them overtaking others that you cannot run at the same speed. In each case, your section of track cannot hold as many trains as it did; whether you have decelerated all, or only some of your trains, you have had to reduce your line capacity. You will find that these difficulties with train lines sloped at differing angles are easier to avoid if your graph covers only a small area of time and distance. The lesson of that is that it is easier to execute a frequent interval service over the comparatively short distances of, say, the Southern Region's electrified lines than over the East Coast main line from London to Newcastle.

I have expanded on these problems of timetabling to hint at the amount of work involved in preparing a timetable such as the Eastern and North Eastern Regions of British Railways hope to introduce in the 1962 summer, with regular on-the-hour departures from King's Cross to Newcastle and trains at 20 minutes past the hour to other destinations, such as the West Riding, York, Hull and Sheffield. I have also endeavoured to show how it would have been much easier with electric traction, but taxed ingenuity because the 'Deltics' are mingled with steam Pacifics and 2,000-h.p. Type 4 diesels, which cannot guarantee the same level of performance. Thus allowance has to be made for the fact that the 'Deltic'-hauled 10 a.m. 'Flying Scotsman' from King's Cross, running on a 6-hour 3-minute timing to Edinburgh, 393 miles distant, would inevitably make faster progress than the preceding 9 a.m. to Newcastle, booked for Pacific or Type 4 diesel haulage, and decrease the line occupation between them. Electric traction would have accelerated the evening suburban traffic from King's Cross, to cite another problem, and enable the evening business expresses to make the same pace back to the West Riding, Newcastle and Tees-side as the morning counterparts up to town, but at present the track capacity in the inner and outer London area between 5 and 6.30 p.m. is not sufficient to permit this.

A locomotive is no use without its train. While the timetable is planned, coaching stock workings must be schemed in just the same detail and with the same concern to diagram for each train set a day's work that will extract from it a healthy revenue-earning mileage. In due course Carriage Rosters are printed showing the precise formation of each train, with the types of vehicle required to make it up, their destinations and their preceding and succeeding duties.

Before greatly accelerated schedules can be agreed, the various engineering branches of the railway must be satisfied. So far as the new locomotives themselves are concerned, practical testing procedure is rather the reverse of that with steam. A steam locomotive, for reasons outlined in Chapter I, is unpredictable. Some of the world's major railway systems – among them British Railways, at Rugby – built stationary testing plants on which their steam locomotives could be run for hours on rollers, in controlled conditions of loading, firing and driving, so that the engineers could assess both the most economic methods of using them and the maximum efforts of which they were capable (sometimes with the use of two firemen simultaneously, on British locomotives not fitted with mechanical stokers). British Railways also built and equipped Mobile Test Units, cleverly devised to exert by electrical means any desired resistance to the locomotive's pull, so that the same controlled testing over lengthy periods could be carried out on the open road. As a result, an immense fund of knowledge on the most efficient use of, and desirable modifications to, many classes of British steam locomotive has been built up.

With a diesel or electric locomotive, the object of testing the performance of the finished product is primarily to ensure it matches up to specifications. One of the most absorbing rail journeys I have made of late was in an Eastern Region dynamometer car when the first one of the East Coast Route 'Deltics', No. D9001, fresh from its builders, was being proved in this way on a special high-speed trial from King's Cross to Doncaster and back with a 375-ton train. The dynamometer car is a special vehicle equipped to measure the pull of a locomotive: its leading coupling, which is attached to the locomotive, is arranged so that the locomotive is pulling against a system of springs and the effort exerted is transcribed continuously on a moving graph in the car. The engineers had worked out beforehand a comprehensive chart of the exact speeds and rates of acceleration the locomotive, when on full power, should achieve with a 375-ton train throughout the run, considering its theoretical performance in relation to the load and gradients; the object of the exercise was largely to compare reality with promise – and fascinating it was to see the predictions fulfilled within a mile or so per hour for mile after mile, seeing that they had been made before No. D9001 had turned a wheel on the track.

Finally, an essential prelude to a faster, more frequent service with diesel or electric traction is civil engineering attention to the track. In Chapter III we observed that the reorganization of old-fashioned junctions and cramped station layouts is a sensible investment that may extract more revenue from the new traction because it facilitates their operation; but in any event all track itself requires strengthening to withstand the different stresses – and the more intensive ones – exerted by the frequent passage of diesel and electric locomotives. The movement of trains inevitably tends to distort the permanent way and the imposition of heavier forces must be met by the renovation of the track with deeper foundations to absorb the load. In recent years traffic operation in Britain has suffered severely from the incessant work of the engineers to this end, which often necessitates their week-end 'possession' of a section or more of main line, round which Sunday trains have to make a tedious diversion by another route.

Efficient drainage is a vital feature of firm track and that is why so much recent British permanent-way work has involved digging out and renewing the foundations themselves, as well as the metals. A factor in good drainage is cleanliness of the ballast supporting the track. Nowadays ballast can be cleaned with the track still in place by a self-contained, self-propelled Matisa ballast-cleaner, which passes an endless bucket chain under the sleepers to scoop out the dirty material; the ballast is sieved of its dirt on the machine and then transferred to a moving belt which discharges it back to the track in a smooth spread. The removal of the dirt will have lightened the ballast, so that after the cleaning some fresh material will have to be added. Then the relaid ballast must be packed solid to keep the track rigid; the modern tool for this job is a self-propelled machine, which pounds rapidly-vibrating tamping tools into the ballast to a depth of some three inches below the bottom of the sleepers and packs the material snugly under the ends of each one of them.

British Railways have at last followed the example of other major world railways and adopted as standard the flat-bottomed rail, secured to the sleepers by elastic spikes through baseplates, instead of the traditional British bullhead-section rail with chairs and keys. The reduced number of fastenings required with flat-bottomed rail makes for a substantial economy, while greater strength and ability to provide a smoother ride are also claimed for it. In these days, track is usually relaid in pre-fabricated lengths from special track-laying trains of various designs. An example is the Morris tracklayer employed in Britain, which can lift a section of old permanent way from a point ahead of it on the line over which it is running, pass the worn length back on a transporter to the rear of its trailing train of flat wagons, and from the front of them bring up a section of new track – again on its transporter system – to drop into the spot it has just cleared.

More and more rails at home and abroad are being welded into lengths of 300ft or more; the record is held by the U.S. Denver & Rio Grande Western Railroad, which has long-welded a continuous stretch of 6·4 miles through its Moffat Tunnel in the Rockies. The passenger, of course, derives the comfort of much less noisy travelling, because the monotonous beat of coach wheels on rail-joints is absent over long-welded track, but to the railway it means a longer life for its track and reduced maintenance costs, since the battering of rail-joints by passing trains is the prime cause of track wear and damage. Special attention has to be paid to the weather conditions at the time long-welded rails are installed, so that it is not done in an unduly high or low temperature when the rails are expanded or contracted to the maximum, or troublesome effects would follow in the opposite extreme of temperature. The inevitable expansion that occurs in hot weather (to allow for which the gaps in unwelded track are left at the fishplate joins between rails) is spread over the whole length of a welded section and largely taken up as an unrelieved stress by the rail itself; but at each end a spliced rail-joint, known as an adjustment or 'breather' switch, allows more freedom of movement than the usual kind, should the rail for any reason expand abnormally. Long-welded track is usually laid on concrete sleepers, which are five times as heavy as the old wooden type and therefore help to maintain the stability of the permanent way by opposing greater resistance to any tendency to move.

104

VI

THE PROBLEM OF THE SUBURBAN PASSENGER PEAKS

ISCUSSING electric traction earlier in this book, we remarked that British Railways were intent on the conversion of suburban lines in their early 25,000-volts a.c. electrification schemes. Why should their resources be squandered on short-distance travellers, one might ask, when the most menacing competition is for long-distance passenger and freight traffic? The answer is that, because no other means of transport can handle the week-day rush-hour crowds – or wants to, since they can be very unprofitable to carry – the railway must seek the most efficient means to move them and cut its operating losses on the exercise. Another spur to modernization of suburban services in Britain is that this is one railway traffic which, in many areas, grows remorselessly as the population spreads round the perimeter of the big towns and cities. Look at a few examples of British suburban railway traffic, both to see the extent of the traffic carried and the impossibility of handling it by any other means.

At the country end of the Eastern Region's Liverpool Street terminus, in London, 18 platforms and two lay-by roads in the centre of the station merge through very complex pointwork into six running lines for the ascent of Bethnal Green bank. By the winter of 1962 no steam trains will be using Liverpool Street and the only non-electrified workings, after the engineers have closed the present Chelmsford–Colchester 'gap' in the conductor wires to permit introduction of a Liverpool Street–Colchester–Clacton multiple-unit service, will be the diesel locomotive-powered expresses to Cambridge and King's Lynn, to Ipswich and Norwich, and down the East Suffolk main line.

Throughout the day there is an intensive interval suburban service on those six tracks out of Liverpool Street. But in the peak hours they are packed to capacity. When the electric multiple-unit service to Clacton has been added to the stream the three outward-bound tracks will be carrying a total of 69 trains in the single hour between 5 and 6 p.m. – 24 on each of the two suburban lines, the easternmost to Ilford, Gidea Park, and Shenfield, the westernmost to the Chingford, Enfield, Hertford and Bishop's Stortford area; and 21 on the centre main-line departure track, which carries the Ipswich and Cambridge main-line expresses, the Clacton and Southend fast multiple-units. On the suburban line leading out of the west side of the station the majority of the departures in this peak hour run at no more than a two-minute headway from their predecessors; on the other suburban line the service is more evenly spread.

Between 5 and 6 p.m. each working day evening, therefore, between 75,000 and 100,000 people will pour out of Liverpool Street on three railway lines whose total width is not more than that of a two-lane motorway. Transfer – in your imagination – this huge number of passengers to road transport and you have the prospect of about five double-decker buses a second hurtling down your motorway; that is impossible to conceive in reality even were such a thing as an unrestricted motorway from the heart of London ever likely to exist. Only the railway can do the peak-hour job, as it does every day in London, not just to and from Liverpool Street, but from the other London termini and on the underground trains of London Transport.

In that same 5–6 p.m. hour, for example, about 80 trains are channelled through the world-famous Clapham Junction of the Southern Region to the southern and south-western suburbs of the capital. A further 53 from the Southern's Cannon Street and Charing Cross stations are taking their turn over the two tracks which are available to thread outward traffic through the key Borough Market Junction – where, incidentally, the path of the trains from Charing Cross cuts right across that of about 30 trains heading for Cannon Street.

To take only one of London Transport's feverishly busy underground lines, during the crucial

Left: Suburban electric multiple-units of the Southern Region of British Railways at London Bridge (Eastern Section).

[*R. C. Riley*

Right: The Kent Coast electrification – a regular interval express formed of three four-car units from Ramsgate and Dover to Victoria near St. Mary Cray.

[*S. Creer*

Below: The evening rush-hour begins at London's Charing Cross terminus, with every platform occupied by Southern suburban electric multiple-units.

[*R. C. Riley*

60 minutes 34 westbound Metropolitan Line trains enter Baker Street station on a single track from the Aldgate and City direction, carrying about 20,000 passengers between them. Of these 34 trains, 18 are bound for the line which diverges here from the underground Circle and heads north for the outer suburbs of Harrow, Uxbridge, Rickmansworth and beyond; these 18 must be cut across the path of 16 trains heading for the City on the Circle line in the opposite direction; and the latter 16 must be merged on that track with 14 more eastbound trains coming off the outer suburban line to make for the City. In all, therefore, the two underground tracks, at Baker Street, are carrying 64 trains between 5 and 6 p.m. On many of the Tube lines of London Transport the headway between trains in the central area of London throughout the morning and evening peaks is as brief as 90 seconds.

Is the suburban passenger – or commuter, to use the American term that has now become colloquial the world over – grateful that railways exist to ferry him to and from his place of business much faster than he could travel by other means (as occasionally he learns bitterly when a labour dispute or technical fault drives him on to the roads for a day or so)? Not he. He will point to a bottleneck like the Southern's Borough Market Junction and ask why it cannot be enlarged, since it is obviously taxed to the limit in the peak-hour. Cattle travel in more comfort than the commuter on many city lines, who rarely finds a seat and often, even when he has to stand, little room to unfold his newspaper. Obviously there should be more trains: if there is not the track capacity to work them, then additional running lines should be laid in. Alternatively, let us have much longer trains, the City man suggests. And, he adds, since the commuter is the railway's most regular customer, day in and day out, is he not entitled to the cheapest season-ticket rates, especially as he is subjected to such discomfort on his morning and evening journeys?

The unpalatable fact is that, despite his constant custom, the suburban season-ticketholder is *not* the railway's best-paying patron – not by a long way. In the years between the wars, when the Southern Railway spread its electrified third-rail around and beyond the southern perimeter of London, the private car was very, very far from being the overpowering competitor for off-peak suburban journeys that it now is, and there was a substantial clientele for the regular-interval suburban and outer suburban service the Southern ran on most of its lines. Today the off-peak suburban traveller, despite wooing by cheap fare facilities, too often drifts to the road; but because more and more people are migrating from inner to outer London and beyond to make their homes, the peak-hour throng of people to and from the city grows – on the Southern Region of British Railways alone, say its officers, at the rate of about 10,000 daily passengers a year at the present time.

The result? The Southern has to maintain a substantial portion of its electric multiple-unit fleet solely to carry the peak-hour crowds; for the rest of the day these train sets lie idle in sidings, not earning a penny towards their keep. On London Transport's Metropolitan Line the percentage of train sets needed only during the rush-hour is as high as 50 per cent. The railway staff has to be maintained at a level adequate to cope with operation of the intensive rush-hour train service and the marshalling of its passengers; but they cannot be employed on piecework rates, so that surplus men can be sent home for the quieter periods of the day. At least one of the Southern's big London termini, Cannon Street, serves little purpose except to process a very heavy peak-hour traffic to and from the City; at other times of the day the business is not enough to justify its upkeep. Some of the 21 platforms of the sprawling Waterloo station could undoubtedly be closed if there was no week-day peak-hour turmoil, when more than 21 tracks could be justified to handle the crowds comfortably.

In other words, a substantial railway capacity in terms of men, stations, track, ultra-modern signalling (to keep the heavy traffic moving swiftly and smoothly) and rolling stock has to be maintained by railways in many of the world's big cities – not just London alone – purely for the rush-hour commuter's benefit. His fares have to cover the cost of upkeep of these facilities every 24 hours for his use in only two two-hour periods of each day. Viewed in that light, it is obvious that a very good case indeed must be made out for the possibility of an increase in *off-peak*, as well as peak-hour traffic, before a railway can consider, say, heavy expenditure on electrification of a suburban service, or the extension of a layout to permit operation of more trains. Not so long ago the Southern Region of British Railways spent £3½ million to extend station platforms and modify the track and signalling on suburban routes of its South Eastern

Division so that it could run longer trains and improve rush-hour travelling conditions; all it achieved was to keep pace with the steady growth of peak-hour travel in that area – off-peak patronage is little changed.

The peak, incidentally, is not merely a suburban traffic problem. It occurs at almost every holiday period, when many members of the public make their only railway journeys of the year, so that a host of extra long-distance trains have to be scheduled. Here again, a large stock of coaches surplus to everyday requirements spend many months of the year vegetating in sidings, earning their keep only in the peak holiday weeks when they are needed to form the supplementary services.

To handle the rush-hour commuters economically, it stands to reason that the railway needs ideally to employ the fewest possible number of trains. The railway must therefore design trains of the highest possible passenger capacity; and it must organize its peak-hour operation so that the trains move as fast as possible. If the tempo of operation can be sufficiently accelerated, it may be possible to turn round one train set in time for two return journeys in the rush-hour, whereas otherwise each return trip would have to be made by a separate unit – and one of the latter would surely be surplus for the rest of the day. Fast operation demands signalling to permit the closest headway between trains consistent with safety and trains themselves capable of a high rate of acceleration from frequent stops. The 277 stations of London Transport's railways, for example, average only 0·83 mile in distance from each other; yet London Transport trains running at 90-second headways manage to average $20\frac{1}{4}$ m.p.h. *inclusive of stops* on their journeys.

The usual modern choice to meet the stipulation of smart acceleration is, of course, the multiple-unit, preferably electric, because of greater operating economy on services of high traffic density and higher accelerative potential. It has a driving cab at each end, so that it can be quickly turned round at terminals; it can satisfy its own power requirements, so that when peak-hour traffic demands longer trains, they are automatically provided with extra power in adequate proportion as fresh units are coupled on; and, whether diesel or electric, the modern multiple-unit can tuck all its power plant under its frames, leaving the maximum room above them for passenger accommodation.

No one has more experience in designing electric multiple-units for commuter traffic of the highest density than London Transport, and its modern Type 'R' stock for London's District Line is an excellent example of modern equipment that is worth closer examination. To secure the high acceleration rate of 1·8 m.p.h. per second from the very frequent and briefly spaced stops of the District Line service, the busiest of the whole L.T. system in the peak hours, the latest 'R' stock vehicles are built of aluminium to minimize weight and every car of the 6- or 8-car trains operated is powered with one 110-h.p. engine in each of its bogies; that means a total output of 1,760 h.p. to move a total of 248 tons' tare weight in an 8-car train, with a capacity for 352 seated passengers and at least as many more standing.

The most efficient and well-equipped multiple-units are not enough in themselves to clear London Transport's rail passengers, which number over $6\frac{1}{2}$ million a year. Before even they reach the trains, Londoners are served with their ticket by machine and speeded down from ground level to underground platforms by fast-moving escalators. Once on the platform, the passengers must be transferred to the trains as quickly as possible; hence each coach has ample door space and air-operated doors under the guard's control. The signalling, which is fully automatic, must be arranged to keep the trains moving safely at a lively speed between stations, but as close to each other as possible. The ingenuities of London Transport's signalling apparatus deserve a chapter to themselves, but I have had the room only to describe their latest development, the programme machine, in Chapter VIII.

Of other underground railways – which are still growing in number; those of Stockholm and Toronto are recent additions and Rotterdam and Milan are building them – New York's is the biggest and the busiest, handling over $1\frac{1}{4}$ million passengers a year at its 482 stations. The Paris Metro, too, deals with more passengers than London Transport, but its stations are very closely spaced, averaging only 525 yards apart, and the average length of journey in the French capital is shorter. One interesting feature of the Paris system is its experiments with rubber-tyred trains, which are in complete command of one short, sharply-curved and steeply graded line. Outside

LONDON TRANSPORT TRAINS

Today's look in London Transport tube trains – a prototype driving motor car built by Cravens. Notice the wide windows and the spacious atmosphere of the fluorescently-lit interior of the car (*left*).

A train of the modern 'R' multiple-unit stock used on the District lines of London Transport. Like the new tube train illustrated above, the vehicles are in an unpainted, metal finish.

This Swiss Federal Railways express, although it is made up to ten coaches, is working push-and-pull and reaches speeds of up to 80 m.p.h.; the locomotive in the foreground is pushing and the train is being driven from a control trailer at the far end. The vehicle with a pantograph in the middle of the train is the restaurant car, which draws current from the overhead wires for cooking purposes.

[*Swiss Federal Railways*

the normal flanged wheels on each bogie of these trains are bigger radius, Michelin-tyred wheels, which rest on flat-surfaced timber rails laid outside the conventional steel running rails. Except when they are negotiating points, the trains ride on these rubber-tyred wheels. At the approach to points, the timber rails slope downwards, lowering the car on its flanged wheels, which make contact with the steel rails and negotiate the pointwork in the usual way, after which the timber rails slope upward to lift the train once more on to its rubber-tyred wheels. Besides its carrying wheels, each bogie has four horizontal wheels, also rubber-tyred, which press laterally on to guide rails laid parallel to and outside the carrying rails, and a trifle higher than the latter. These guide rails are also the conductor rails, from which collector shoes on the train pick up the current in the normal way. (To limit the size of the tunnels, third-rail current pick-up is usual underground; Rome's neat little system, opened as recently as 1955 and about to be extended, is exceptional for its overhead conductor wires.) The French claim that the rubber tyres, besides making for quieter running, vastly improve the adhesion of the motor bogies, enhancing acceleration and braking, so that journey times on steeply graded routes can be cut and line capacity increased.

For surface commuter lines the multiple-unit is by no means the exclusive present-day choice of the world's railways. In recent years we have seen some striking developments of a practice which in Britain we tend, without reason, to regard as old-fashioned – the push-and-pull train. The push-and-pull is locomotive-powered, but the train formation is provided with an additional driving cab at the outer end of the endmost coach and there are means, mechanical or electrical, either for the locomotive to be driven from this distant cab, as is usual nowadays, or else for the driver to impart driving instructions to a colleague on the locomotive, who manipulates its controls as requested. Thus the locomotive and train are reversible intact; the locomotive can pull or push its train and need not run round the coaches at each terminal, but, whether it is at the front or rear, it can always be controlled from the head of the train.

In Britain the push-and-pull is obsolescent. Antiquated Ministry of Transport regulations restrict the number of passenger-occupied coaches that can be pushed to two, so that the push-and-pull has never been of value except on rural branch lines; and today branches that are considered to have a chance of running profitably are undergoing dieselization with multiple-units, and the less promising are being shut down.

Go no farther abroad than Paris, however, and you will encounter push-and-pull working on a scale never seen in Britain. For years some of the Paris surface suburban services have been operated by 8-coach, steam 2–8–2 tank-powered trains of this kind, with the locomotives equipped

110

for remote control by the most modern electro-pneumatic means. In the Paris area of the 25,000 volts a.c.-electrified Lille main line, 8-coach commuter services are safely propelled at speeds of up to 60 m.p.h. by 3,600-h.p. electric locomotives, which, of course, are much more conveniently arranged for remote electro-pneumatic operation from the opposite end of their trains through control cables running the length of the coaches. These latter French commuter trains have all the quick turnround capability of a multiple-unit, but the advantage that their motive power is independent, so that it can be employed on other work, notably freight, outside the peak hours.

The Great Northern Line of the Eastern Region of British Railways similarly uses diesel locomotives on a proportion of its London commuter workings, so that they can be diverted to cross-London freight haulage in the off-peak period; but, as I have explained, the G.N. Line cannot go to the same lengths as the French and avoid tiresome shunting movements in the cramped area of King's Cross terminus by operating its London–Hitchin–Cambridge trains on push-and-pull principles – British regulations forbid it. Diesel locomotives are just as convenient for this practice as electric locomotives; the German Federal Railway makes increasing use of its medium-power diesels in this way and has lately been building new push-and-pull driving trailer coaches of very modern design.

That the British restrictions are outdated is demonstrated spectacularly by present-day Swiss exploitation of push-and-pull working on high-speed inter-city services. For some years the Swiss Federal Railways have run 7-coach push-and-pull expresses from Lucerne to Zürich and to Berne. In mid-1959 the practice was extended to more routes and some of the country's fastest expresses, which were handed over to new push-and-pull train sets of as many as 10 and 12 coaches. Some of these are powered by 2,580-h.p. electric locomotives, others by remarkable 2,800-h.p. motor-coaches, which manage to find room for 69 passenger seats as well as their power plant in a mere 63 tons of vehicle. These lengthy Swiss push-and-pull trains are often propelled at speeds as fast as 80 m.p.h. in order to maintain their mile-a-minute timings between intermediate stops.

One of the newest recruits to push-and-pull operation of commuter trains, the Chicago & North Western of the U.S.A. (which uses diesel locomotives), is also one of the several world systems that has boosted the seating capacity of each commuter car by adopting double-decker vehicles. A number of the other double-decker operators are American, but France, Germany, Czechoslovakia and Poland are European countries which have managed to find room within their loading gauges for extensive use of suburban coaches with two seating levels. The generous coach proportions allowable in the U.S.A. permit the Chicago & North Western to pack seats

A push-and-pull train of the French National Railways, working on the suburban services from the Gare du Nord terminus, Paris; the locomotive is a 3,650 h.p. unit, No. BB–16505, working on the 25,000 volts a.c. system.
[C. P. Boocock

U.S. suburban passenger equipment – a double-decker, diesel locomotive-powered
suburban train of the Chicago & North Western Railway showing (*left*) the driving-
cab end of the control trailer and (*right*) the interior of one of the cars, in which the
upper galleries are reached by stairways from the centre entrance vestibule; and
(*right*) a typical American city subway train, in this case one of the Philadelphia
Subway units.

for 160 into each of the 55-ton, two-storey cars with which they have recently modernized their
Chicago commuter services.

In 1949 the Southern Region of British Railways introduced two 4-car multiple-units that
were the nearest the British loading gauge permitted to double-deckers. One upper compartment was dovetailed with two lower ones throughout the length of each vehicle, but the upper
compartments were too high above the ground to be furnished with their own doors and they
had to be reached through the compartments downstairs. This proved a troublesome operating
snag. Whereas 507 passengers could be seated in each 4-car unit, compared with the 375 or
400 of the conventional Southern set, it took too long to load and unload them, because of the
smaller proportion of compartment doors to passenger seats in the double-deckers; consequently,
instead of moving rush-hour passengers faster, the double-deckers were slowing up their handling
at intermediate stations. The two units are still at work on North Kent suburban services, but
experience with these prototypes decided the Southern against multiplying them and in favour
of a costly programme of station, track and signalling alterations to permit the operation of
longer trains of orthodox single-deck multiple-units.

The French National Railways' "Mistral" between Paris, Lyons, Marseilles and Nice. Headed by an electric locomotive as far as Avignon, it averages 64.8 m.p.h. throughout the 674.7 miles between Paris and Nice, nine intermediate stops included

[Blocks courtesy of J. Stone & Co. [Deptford] Ltd.

A German Federal Railway 'Trans-Europe Express' diesel-hydraulic unit on the 'Parsifal' service, alongside the Oise river between Compiègne and Noyon, in France

[Y. Broncard

An Italian 'Trans-Europe Express' diesel unit skirts the French Riviera coast between Cannes and St. Raphael on the Milan–Marseilles 'Ligure' service

[Y. Broncard

VII

SPEEDING THE FREIGHT

MOST of the world's major railway systems carry vastly more car-loads of freight than they do of passengers; and most of them are therefore dependent chiefly on their goods traffic for prosperity – particularly in North America, where competition has drained off the railways' passengers so disastrously. It follows that modernization of railways has paid particular attention to the means of freight movement.

The chief competitor, the road vehicle, scores through its flexibility of operation. It is available whenever it is needed; it can travel straight from starting point to destination without being side-tracked *en route*, as a railway wagon sometimes is for shunting from one train to another in a marshalling yard; and – most important – it conveys its load from door to door, without any intermediate handling. True, there are limitations to the kind of traffics road vehicles can conveniently carry; they are not ideal for the transport of heavy minerals, for example. This might be a crumb of comfort were it not that in some parts of the world – especially Western Europe – some of the traffics for which railways are particularly suited have slumped in recent years.

Coal is the biggest of these disappointments. In many industrial uses it has been supplanted by oil; and in domestic use it is yielding to electricity, which has meant changes in the pattern of coal distribution from the pits, from widespread dispersal to private consumers to more compact hauls to power stations. To offset their losses of coal traffic, many railways – our own foremost amongst them – have launched a fierce struggle, not only to keep the merchandise traffic they have, but to wrest back from the road much that has been lost in the post-war period. To achieve this the road hauliers must be beaten on their own ground – door-to-door transit at times to suit the consignor's convenience. Some of the most interesting rail-freight developments in recent years have been moves in this contest.

The greatest advances have been made in North America, for a number of reasons. First, the spur of competition has been strongest. Second, the distances in that vast country over which the goods are carried lengthens the economic advantages of rail over road for trunk freight haulage, for the costs of rail operation decrease as the mileage increases. As a result, the North American railways have a margin to spend on the purchase and maintenance of special rolling stock to facilitate door-to-door transport. Finally, the design of this rolling stock is made easier by the generosity of the North American loading gauge. The U.S. and Canadian railways, therefore, have been encouraged to pursue 'piggy-back' methods on a large scale.

'Piggy-back' marries the natural advantages of road and rail. A road vehicle, which is usually a tractor and trailer, picks up the goods from the consignor's premises and makes for the nearest railhead. There the trailer, with or without its wheels still in place, is loaded on to a rail vehicle for a 'piggy-back' ride on the main section of its journey across country, where rail transport is cheaper, faster and – in the case of many manufactured goods – safer, because the freight rides more smoothly and is less liable to damage; for this last reason American railroads are building up a big business in the 'piggy-backing' of new automobiles from the manufacturer to dealer. At another railhead close to its consignee, the trailer is replaced on road; and a road tractor is once more called up to carry out the job for which it is best suited – the local delivery to the recipient's doorstep. (Incidentally, the Germans reverse this last stage in many industrial areas by rolling rail wagons on to a low slung frame with road wheels and hauling them through the streets to their destination!).

By these means the railways show the road haulier a clean pair of heels; they offer the same door-to-door facilities, but because so much of the journey is by rail it is completed faster. One essential to speed, of course, is a swift and easy means of getting the road trailer on and off the 'piggy-backing' rail vehicle. Most U.S. railroads employ trains of 85ft-long flat cars, each of which has room for two conventional road trailers; the gaps between the cars are boarded over and the tractors can propel their trailers straight on to and along the train to their required position, where the trailers are detached and clamped down, after which the tractors reverse off the train.

Even in the U.S.A., however, it is not every railway that has clearances sufficient to pass a low-slung flat car with a wheeled road box trailer of normal dimensions on top of it. Some systems have had to increase clearances on routes traversed by heavy 'piggy-back' traffic, while the Boston & Maine and the Canadian Pacific have even gone to the extreme of singling track through five-mile tunnels and re-aligning it so that the 'piggy-back' trains can take advantage of the maximum height underneath the crown of the bore. Other railroads have developed equipment which does not require the full height of a wheeled road vehicle to be accommodated above the railcar's frame. There are various versions of a basic idea which cuts away or depresses portions of the railcar floor; the wheels of the road trailer either hang below the frames of the rail vehicle, while the latter's rear axle rest on the centre sill of the wagon: or else the trailer's rear wheels are 'pouched' in slots below the wagon's frame level – the French, who originated this method, call such wagons 'kangaroos'. Then there is the 'Flexi-Van', devised by the New York Central, which is essentially a demountable road trailer body that slides off its axles; the road tractor pushes the body off its axles across the centre of a flat car specially fitted with a turntable that one man can rotate easily, so as to turn the trailer body through 90 degrees into alignment with the wagon.

Since 'piggy-backing' was first practised on a large scale in 1955, U.S. railroads have more than trebled their carryings by these methods. Some systems assert that 90 per cent of their 'piggy-back' traffic was formerly going by road all the way; experts calculate that on the average of the whole country, three-quarters of it is business won back from the roads. Some 'piggy-back' traffic indeed, is still under the flag of road hauliers, who freely concede the railways' greater speed and efficiency in long-distance operation by arranging for their own trailers to be 'piggy-backed', because it is cheaper than providing their own tractors and drivers.

'Piggy-back' devices do not beat the road on their own, however. To enhance their attraction the U.S. railroads have screwed up their merchandise freight operation to the fastest speed in the world. Their current freight-train schedules show more than 100 trains a day with point-to-point timings of 50 m.p.h. average or better over a total of nearly 14,000 miles. The nation's crack transcontinental freight train is the 'Blue Streak Merchandise' of the Southern Pacific, which runs the whole 2,447 miles from St. Louis, Ill. to Los Angeles at an average of 47·1 m.p.h. and reels off much of its itinerary at a mile a minute. For the first time anywhere in the world, one U.S. railroad now has a freight train with a 60 m.p.h. schedule over one section of its journey; this is the New York Central and the train is one of six fast-running trains carrying exclusively 'piggy-back' traffic, two linking New York and Chicago (and covering the 900-odd miles in 20½ hours), two Boston and Albery, and two Cleveland and St. Louis.

'Piggy-back', the newest and most promising development in rail-freight operation, is spreading elsewhere in the world, even where loading gauges are more restrictive. French railways, for example, now run nightly trains of their 'Kangaroo' wagons from Paris to Bordeaux and to Toulouse, with a coach included in the formation to accommodate the lorry drivers, who can sleep the journey through and wake up refreshed on arrival to drive their vehicle off the train and away from the railhead to its destination. Even in Britain there is coming a 'piggy-back' device of which some railwaymen speak with more excitement than many modernization developments. It is aptly known as the 'Roadrailer', since it can run either on road or rail; and therein lies one gain, for it does not involve the expense of two vehicles, one for each 'medium', as do the U.S. methods already described. Practically self-contained, it is amphibious. Most important, it promises much lower overhead costs of merchandise conveyance – first, because the ratio of the load it can carry to its own basic weight is high; and second, because its availability for both road and rail working will enable a very high utilisation.

The 'Roadrailer' has been developed by its manufacturers, Pressed Steel, and British Railways engineers from the 'Railvan' invented by a U.S. railroad, the Chesapeake & Ohio. Basically, it is a conventional road trailer, but at the rear it has two pairs of retractable wheels, one pair

AMERICAN 'PIGGYBACK'

Right: A 'piggyback' haul of conventional road trailers on the Western Pacific R.R. Note the length of the railroad flat cars.

[*Western Pacific*

Centre: New motor cars are delivered by piggyback. These Studebaker Larks were hauled over road from South Bend, Ind. to Cicero, Ill, where the road trailers carrying them were put on rail cars for haulage by the Burlington Lines to Denver *en route* to Salt Lake City. Two days were saved by comparison with all-road delivery methods.

[*Burlington Lines*

Bottom: 'Flexi-vans' (see *page* 114) on the Milwaukee Road. One man can rotate the body on its flat car mounting to transfer it from road to rail or vice versa.

[*Milwaukee Road*

115

BRITISH RAILWAYS' 'ROADRAILER'

[*Trains Illustrated Photos.*]

The 'Roadrailer' arrives at the road-rail transfer point with rail wheels retracted. Note the simplicity of the undercarriage gear. . . .

. . . It is positioned over the rails by the road tractor. Now compressed air is connected to the motor to retract road wheels and lower rail wheels . . .

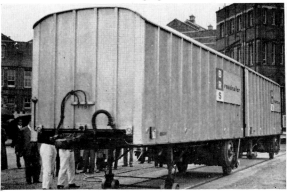

. . . Two 'Roadrailers' are coupled, ready for a rail journey. Note the plug and socket coupling . .

. . The platform of the adaptor vehicle slides neatly under the body of the 'Roadrailer' . . .

. . . The adaptor vehicle is brought up by a B.R./Sulzer Type '2' diesel. The socket coupling is conspicuous . . .

. . . and seconds later the diesel is ready to haul the 'Roadrailers' out of the yard on to the main line.

for road and one for rail; each axle can be raised or lowered independently by compressed air, like the undercarriage of an aircraft. All that is needed to make a siding suitable for the transfer of a 'Roadrailer' from one method of travel to another is to build the ballast up to a firm surface at rail level. An ordinary road tractor brings the 'Roadrailer' in from its consignor and positions it over the track, then unhooks in the normal way and retires. The yard staff now bring up a portable air compressor to lower the vehicle's rail wheels on to the track, after which its road wheels can be lifted. Within seconds it is ready for rail travel. On its own and stationary the 'Roadrailer' is supported at the front by dolly wheels; but in movement it is a two-wheeled vehicle. It couples to its neighbour by a plug-and-socket device that takes the weight of the trailer's front end, enabling the dolly wheels to be raised; thus, in a 'Roadrailer' train each vehicle is resting on the one in front – and the leading vehicle on a special adaptor bogie, with a 'Roadrailer' coupling at one end and a conventional B.R. coupling at the other, which must be inserted to marry the train to its locomotive.

Obviously, the 'Roadrailer' cannot be used economically as a general-service freight wagon. The B.R. aim is to run exclusively 'Roadrailer' trains between railheads in the major industrial centres without any intermediate stops for remarshalling; the 'Roadrailers' may be B.R.-owned, or the property of outside firms which B.R. agree to run in their 'Roadrailer' trains. These trains

 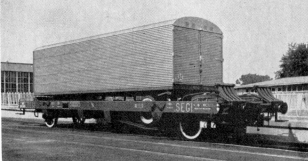

For door-to-door deliveries to some customers without rail access to their premises, the German Federal Railway employs road trailers on to which rail vans can be mounted bodily for road haulage from the railhead nearest to their final destination.

The French Railways use the 'Kangaroo'-type wagon for their piggyback traffic. The wagon gets its name because the rear wheels of the road trailer can be 'pouched' beneath the frames of the wagon, thereby reducing the overall height of the loaded wagon and easing clearance problems.

may be as many as 75 'Roadrailers' long and run at up to 70 m.p.h., for the 'Roadrailer' has been proved quite stable at speeds as high as 85 m.p.h. In the future its employment may extend beyond the carriage of merchandise in box bodies, for such variants as a tanker 'Roadrailer' are being developed. So far, 50 have been ordered by B.R. for service trials.

Hitherto, British Railways' chief weapon in the door-to-door duel with road transport has been the container, which can be transferred bodily between road and rail vehicles without any intermediate handling of the merchandise in it. The containers have been produced in a wide variety of sizes and for all manner of commodities, from bricks and pipes to furniture and frozen foods, including ice-cream (for which, of course, they must be highly insulated to maintain a low temperature within). The disadvantage of containers, by comparison with the 'Roadrailer', is that the transfer point must be provided with a crane or other lifting device to trans-ship them. Another method which reduces to the minimum the time-wasting handling of goods in transit at railway depots is 'palletization' – the stacking of goods on inverted 'U'-form platforms, called pallets, which can be moved speedily from road vehicle to rail van by fork-lift trucks. Many famous household goods packed in cartons are palletized by their manufacturers and travel that way throughout their B.R. journeys.

British Railways freight trains – (*left*) a fast merchandise train of the Eastern Region sets out from London for the North behind Class 'V2' 2–6–2 No. 60855; and (*below*) Class "9F" 2–10–0 No. 92102 passes Kenton, in the London suburbs on the L.M.R., with a haul of special bogie hopper wagons used for block train working of coal between pits and a London power station.

[*K. L. Cook, D. Cross*

Here again, however, containers and palletization do not win traffic on their own. Every year more of British Railways' merchandise freight trains are being run at express speeds. On the East Coast Route a number of the crack merchandise trains are included in the duties of the top enginemen and locomotives at depots like King's Cross, London, and Gateshead or Heaton on Tyneside – trains like the 8 p.m. 'Tees–Tyne Freighter' from King's Cross, which the time-table requires to average $43\frac{1}{2}$ m.p.h. throughout the $185\frac{3}{4}$ miles from Finsbury Park, London, to York, inclusive of a stop at Peterborough to change enginemen; or the 3.5 p.m. from King's Cross to Niddrie yard, Edinburgh, which is booked to be overtaken by the fast passenger King's Cross–Edinburgh 'Talisman' before Peterborough, but which has been known after that to catch the 'Talisman' up and suffer a signal check as a result! On the other side of the country the London Midland Region's 'Condor' offers an overnight transit of traffic in containers each way between Hendon, in the London suburbs, and Gushetfaulds goods depot, Glasgow, running the $402\frac{1}{4}$ miles in just under 10 hours with only one intermediate stop at Carlisle; the 'Condor' is booked to be hauled by Type '2' diesel locomotives, which work throughout between London

and Glasgow, for when the train is diesel-powered only the enginemen are changed at Carlisle.

Until 1955, two snags prevented the railways of Britain from accelerating the general level of their freight traffic operation. The most important of these was that, almost alone of the world's major railway systems, we had not standardized continuous braking on our freight stock. Most of our wagon stock was equipped only with handbrakes, so that the only braking power on the majority of freight trains was that available on the locomotive and the brakevan; consequently, 25-30 m.p.h. was the *highest* speed these vehicles could be safely allowed on the main line, compared with the respective point-to-point *averages* of 40 and 50 m.p.h. permitted a Class 'D' freight train, on which at least a third of the wagons are vacuum-brake-fitted for control from the locomotive, and a Class 'C', which must consist of vacuum brake-fitted wagons for at least four-fifths of its length. The 1955 Modernization Plan, however, envisaged the equipment of the whole British Railways wagon stock with vacuum brakes. The programme has been under way for a considerable period and the entire fleet of merchandise wagons is now brake-fitted, so that an enormous increase in the number of Class 'C' and 'D' freights run daily has been possible over the past few years. Moreover, an increasing variety of wagons is now equipped with

Three stages in the transit of a container in British Railways – (*left*) by road vehicle from consignor to railhead; (*centre*) during transfer from road to rail, in the hands of the 'Freightlifter', a useful item of goods depot equipment which can be employed as a fork-lift truck or a crane; and (*right*) loaded on to flat trucks for haulage from railhead to railhead, in this case by Brush Type '2' diesel-electric locomotive No. D5535.

[*British Railways*

continuous brakes, enlarging the range of goods that travel by fast freight services; for example British Railways' big share of the post-war oil trade from refineries to storage depots has been partly won by the provision of new high-capacity, brake-fitted tank wagons. But the great majority of mineral wagons, unfortunately, still lack vacuum brakes and many will remain so for years because the railways are short of money to convert them.

At this juncture it should be mentioned that British Railways also differ from most of the principal world railways (the more important of Britain's companions are Denmark, Norway, Spain, South Africa, India and Japan) in employing the vacuum, instead of the air brake, on locomotive-hauled and diesel – but not electric – multiple-unit stock. Briefly the vacuum system applies train brakes by admitting air to the continuous pipe running the length of the train and connected between vehicles; exhausters are required to maintain a vacuum in the pipe and hold the brakes off when the train is running. Air brakes work conversely; when the train is running, full air pressure must be maintained in the train pipe, but when the driver reduces this by opening his brake-valve, compressed air is allowed to pass from reservoirs on each vehicle to the latter's brake cylinders and apply the brakes. The only attraction of the vacuum brake nowadays is that its apparatus is cheaper than a compressed air system, for on the score of efficiency the air brake undoubtedly wins; it is quicker acting – especially in release – and less sensitive to

A CONTRAST
IN WAGON SIZE —
U.S. AND BRITISH

Recent British and American prototypes of maximum capacity tank wagons demonstrate strikingly the possibilities of size afforded by the loading gauges and other clearances on each side of the Atlantic.

The British prototype (*left*), built by Charles Roberts of Horbury, near Wakefield, is a four-wheeler with an overall length of 27 ft. 1½ in. on the 15-ft. wheelbase most appropriate to high speed tank wagons used on British Railways; the capacity of its tank barrel, the largest which the British loading gauge allows on a 15-ft. wheelbase, is 7,500 gallons. By contrast, the U.S. car, appropriately nicknamed a 'Hot Dog', can carry 23,400 gallons of petrol; it is 85 ft. long and fully loaded weighs 112 tons, against the 40 tons of the British vehicle.

leakage in the train pipe, because it works at a higher pressure. Many engineers hold that when they began to modernize, British Railways should have taken the opportunity to follow those systems which have turned from vacuum to air braking in recent decades; British Railways' not entirely convincing answer is that it would have disrupted their operations to have withdrawn all their existing coaches and brake-fitted wagons for conversion, even if the work had been done by batches of stock over a lengthy period.

British Railways were also handicapped by the prevalence of grease-lubricated wagons amongst the rolling stock they inherited after 1948, because of such vehicles' greater proneness to overheating. These wagons have now been eliminated from the fleet, but even so the occurrence of 'hot boxes' with normal oil-lubricated plain bearings is much more of a problem with freight than with passenger trains, because wagons inevitably do not receive the same standard of maintenance – including lubricant attention – as passenger vehicles. U.S. railroads are so concerned with the 'hot box' as a brake on the efficiency of their freight operation that a growing number are installing 'hot box' detectors at strategic points, such as sections of main line on which trains are likely to make their maximum pace. These detectors, which are beamed on passing trains at axlebox level, are sensitive to heat and are arranged with electronic devices to advise a control point ahead and to place signals automatically at danger, so that a train is halted for examination, if they sense that the heat emanating from any axlebox is above the safety level. They are cleverly designed to ignore confusion from overheated brake-blocks. The most refined of these detectors count the axleboxes as they pass and pinpoint the delinquent's position on the train, forwarding the information to the control point ahead so that the train staff do not have to waste time searching for the wagon in trouble.

One way of overcoming 'hot box' tendencies is to substitute more expensive types of axlebox for plain bearings. The most widely employed alternative is the roller bearing which, as its name suggests, encircles the axle with small rollers that are sealed in a casing which is impenetrable by grit and dust; thus the oil in the bearing is kept free of matter that affects its efficiency – and, moreover, the rollers circulate it evenly over the bearing, thereby preventing overheating. Another type of axlebox which achieves the same result is the Athermos, employing a fan device to spread the lubricant efficiently and avoid the development of excessive frictional heat at any point. British Railways are equipping a growing number of their wagons with axleboxes of these kinds, which can safely be left unexamined for lengthy periods after each servicing with lubricant, and which can be run at high speeds without danger of overheating. They are distinguished by colour circles on their exterior casings, the colour denoting to the staff the particular brand of axlebox.

Another major difference between British Railways' wagon fleet and those of most other major world systems is the size of vehicle. In Europe, for example, although it is true Continental railways operate more bogie freight wagons than our own, the vast majority of goods vehicles are, like ours, four-wheelers; but, generally speaking, the length of a Continental four-wheeler is about half as much again as that of a British one. Continental railways, too, are for the most part laid out to deal in longer trains than British Railways; thus, whereas the average net load of a B.R. freight train works out at no more than 145 tons, in France it is 435 and in Western Germany 455 tons. British Railways are keen to save money by carrying their freight, especially minerals, more economically in fewer wagons – in other words, by providing bigger vehicles of higher capacity, but they are frustrated by the layout characteristics of many yards through which the wagons must pass, especially those in private industrial premises, which it is beyond their power to remodel except by persuading the owners to rebuild. The $24\frac{1}{2}$-ton capacity all-steel mineral wagon introduced by B.R. since 1955 is the very largest possible on a four-wheel underframe, but a limit has had to be placed on the number ordered because they are too massive to negotiate the curves and clearances of the layouts in many industrial plants.

For average size of wagon and length of train the North American railroads stand alone. Bogie freight cars are the rule on all major U.S. systems. As for the size of trains, this can be guessed by comparing, say, the average trainload figure of 2,750 tons for a predominantly coal-carrying combine like the recently merged Norfolk & Western-Virginian system, or even the 1,340-ton average of a less specialist road like the Union Pacific, with the best European results previously quoted. It is by no means infrequent for U.S. freight trains to be made up to more than 100 bogie cars a mile or more in length, with the result that several systems provide radio-telephones to keep the train crewmen in the diesel locomotive in touch with their colleagues far away in the caboose, or brakevan, at the rear of these monster hauls; on some systems the train crewmen are also in radio-telephonic communication with control points at the lineside. Compared with the $24\frac{1}{2}$-ton capacity B.R. mineral wagon, a normal U.S. bogie mineral car can carry up to 70 or 80 tons, with the result that, fully loaded, it will gross in the region of 100 tons, and a 100-car mineral train will run into five figures of tonnage. In fact, 10,000-ton trains are everyday affairs on the chief coal or mineral-carrying systems like the Norfolk & Western-Virginian and the Duluth, Missabe & Iron Range. The D.M. & I.R., indeed, claims that its maximum train-loadings have risen as high as 19,000 tons; a tenth of that tonnage is well beyond the British conception of a really heavy coal train, which would be little more than 1,500 tons.

The modern method of unloading cement in bulk is by air pressure, which transfers the cement by pipeline from a 'Presflo' wagon to a road lorry. The 'Presflo' is a brake-fitted, pressurised, air-slide wagon which carries its load in a completely enclosed all-steel container, pressurised to prevent the cement consolidating as a result of the vibrations when the wagon is in transit. The wagon is loaded by gravity and at the receiving end of its journey the cement is discharged by air pressure at a rate of a ton every $1\frac{1}{4}$ mins, using either a stationary compressed air supply or a portable air compressor.

[British Railways

NEW IDEAS IN CONTINENTAL GOODS WAGONS

Top left: a compressed air-operated, side-tipping wagon of the German Federal Railway. *Top right:* a German Federal Railway hopper wagon, arched so that a road lorry can be backed underneath it to receive its contents. *Centre left:* another type of German Federal hopper wagon, with individually tipping bins. *Centre right:* one of several types of sliding-roof wagon now employed by European railways. *Bottom left:* a German Federal Railway hopper wagon, both ends of which can be raised by compressed air to discharge through the centre of the frames. *Bottom right:* a Swedish Railways van with sliding side walls.

[German Federal Railway, Swedish Railways

One aspect of freight handling in which Western European railways have progressed farther than the North Americans is the evolution of specialist wagons to expedite freight transits or to increase the utilization of wagons. Apart from 'piggy-back' devices already discussed, U.S. railroads, with their large fleets of conventional box cars and 'gondolas', as they term what we call an open wagon, have few novelties to display – unlike, in particular, the German Federal Railway, which no longer builds or orders any open freight vehicles of traditional design.

Nowadays most large industries lay out their railway facilities for the bottom-door discharge of mineral traffic on their premises to avoid time-wasting manual work; the wagons, often of hopper design, are placed on a staith so that they can disgorge their cargo through floor doors into a receptacle below rail level. (In Britain the old North Eastern Railway, because coal was its main business, had the sense to lay out all its coal unloading facilities in this way, even at wayside stations: hence hopper wagons today abound more on the N.E.R. than on any other Region of British Railways.) Where bottom-door discharge is still not possible, the German Federal Railway employs an open wagon whose whole body can be raised off the frames by a hydraulic mechanism and then tipped sideways through 45 degrees to unload its minerals through side doors. A most peculiar-looking mineral wagon with which the Germans are experimenting is one whose body is arched, so that a road vehicle can be backed astride the track underneath it; the wagon's contents can now be emptied straight into the lorry. Increasingly popular now with the French and German railways is a wagon that can be made open or closed according to need; it is basically a high-sided open wagon, but the top can be covered over at will by a collapsible metal shutter that is rather like an outsize, horizontal venetian blind. The Western and Scottish Regions of British Railways are to operate wagons of this type experimentally.

British Railways' wagon innovations have been mainly directed towards the acceleration of freight transit from consignor to consignee by cutting out handling of the goods *en route*. An increasingly familiar sight on British rails nowadays, for example, is the 'Presflo' cement wagon. The bodywork of the wagon is a completely enclosed all-steel container, which is pressurized to prevent the cement consolidating by reason of the wagon's vibration when it is on the move. The cement is funnelled into the wagon by gravity at the producer's works, but it is unloaded by air pressure, without human handling; it is blown through a pipeline either into a storage silo or into a similarly equipped road vehicle, which will in turn discharge the cement by air pressure at the building site where it is needed. Similar air-pressure discharge wagons have been developed for other powered commodities, such as salt and limestone dust.

One of most interesting uses of Presflo wagons – which are equipped with continuous brakes – is in the longest through freight-train working on British Railways. More than half the country's cement output is produced on Thames-side, in the London, Tilbury & Southend Line territory of the Eastern Region. Each weekday morning a train of loaded Presflos is dispatched from Purfleet and travels through without any intermediate re-marshalling to Edinburgh via the East Coast main line; in the Edinburgh area the Presflos are divided into sections for Cambuslang and Leith. The Presflo train runs at Class 'C' speeds and completes its journey of about 400 miles in 16 hours.

This Anglo-Scottish Presflo service exemplifies the most efficient kind of freight-train working, which every railway is anxious to practise as much as possible – the 'block load', run as far as possible without time-wasting halts in marshalling yards to pick up additional wagons or put off some of its vehicles for distribution to their destinations by other freight trains. A wagon in a marshalling yard is making no progress towards its destination and losing ground in the race with road transport. The modern railway, therefore, sets out to devise as many 'block load' operations as it can and to restrict its marshalling yards to the minimum, strategically siting those it must have so that they are convenient for the receipt and dispatch of feeder services from a wide industrial area. For example, the North Eastern Region of British Railways will in a few years have concentrated the larger part of its freight marshalling on only four yards – at Lamesley, on the East Coast main line south of Newcastle, to cater for Tyneside and the Blaydon area; at Thornaby, to deal with the massive Tees-side and Durham traffic; at Stourton, to cover the area to the south and east of Leeds; and at Healey Mills, on the Calder Valley main line west of Leeds, to sort the heavy flows of traffic across the Pennines between the North-East and the West and North-West.

 [*Continued on page* 126]

THIS PAGE:

Above: An aerial view of the huge Conway yard, Pittsburgh, of the Pennsylvania Railroad, U.S.A. Westbound trains to be sorted are received on the tracks in the right foreground, from which they are propelled over a hump into the sorting sidings in the right background. The layout is duplicated, but reversed, for eastbound traffic and the two humps are side by side; the eastbound sorting sidings are on the left.

MODERN MARSHALLING

Right: A close-up of a group of wagon-braking retarders in Conway yard.

[*Pennsylvania Railroad*

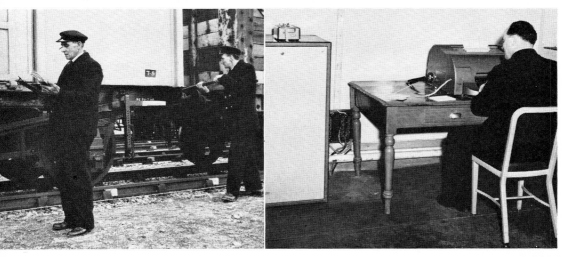

Another inducement to reduce the number of marshalling yards is that this is the age of automated shunting. However, the complex electronic equipment of a modern yard is extremely expensive and to justify outlay on these devices the yard must be one that will be busy day and night, receiving and making up a continuous flow of trains. This is the case with all the major automated yards which British Railways contemplate in their Modernization Plan. Of these, Thornton Junction, Temple Mills, Ripple Lane and Margam have been finished at the time of writing. The most intricate of these is Margam, on the doorstep of the South Wales steel industry, which boasts the most modern equipment in Europe (though there are a large and growing number of similarly endowed yards in the U.S.A.; by 1960 the total had reached 50, topped by the Pennsylvania Railroad's massive Conway yard at Pittsburgh, with 107 sorting sidings of 12,000 bogie freight cars' capacity.)

The 12 reception tracks at Margam are laid out so that trains can be accepted from any direction and their locomotives can be released to the depot or their next duty without crossing the tracks on which marshalling operations are taking place. While this is going on the yard's Traffic Office wants to know as quickly as possible how the train is to be broken up. It gets this information from a shunter who walks the length of the train, reading off the wagons' destinations into a portable radio transmitter. His report is picked up in the Traffic Office, where a traffic clerk transcribes it as a teleprint message, showing the sorting siding to which each 'cut' of the train is to be shunted, according to its destination, and the number of wagons in each 'cut'. Simultaneously, the machine on which the clerk types the teleprint produces a copy of the 'cut' list in code perforations on a tape.

Before following the marshalling procedure at Margam to its next stage, I ought to mention that this first step is one in which the American railroads often make one of their now numerous uses of closed-circuit television. In the U.S.A. the make-up, or 'consist', of a freight train is teleprinted ahead of it from its originating yard. The recipient yard has a television camera at its entrance, beamed at the level of the large running numbers the Americans favour on their freight stock. The traffic clerk sits in front of a T.V. receiver, reading off the car numbers as they pass the camera, and his remarks are tape-recorded; as soon as he has finished the tape is played back as a check against the advance teleprint and, if it agrees, shunting moves already decided can be put into immediate effect.

Now back to Margam. The Traffic Office is ready to sort our incoming train and the perforated tape made by the clerk's teleprinter is fed into a tape reader that governs the whole marshalling operation. Margam, of course, is a hump yard; trains are sorted by propulsion over the single-track humps, from which the 'cuts' into which they have been uncoupled fall away by gravity into one of the 50 sorting sidings appropriate to their destinations. All the route-resetting between 'cuts', to direct each one to its correct siding, is automatically controlled by electronic gadgetry that is set in motion by the tape-reader.

The Traffic Office at Margam is on the ground floor of the Control Tower. On the top floor is the Control Room, surveying the 178 acres of the yard through its wide, deep windows. At the front of the room is the operating desk, on which the yard layout is depicted diagrammatically with thumb switches and push-buttons at the relevant positions on the diagram for manual route-setting of the reception tracks by the operators. The desk also carries a series of push-buttons, numbered from 1 to 50 to correspond with the sorting sidings, by which the operator can set up manually the route from the hump to each siding. Normally, however, all the operator does is to watch that the electronic apparatus carries out correctly its route-setting functions without any intervention on his part.

As soon as the tape is fed into the Traffic Office reader, illuminated panels upstairs on the Control Room desk display in order the numbers of the first four sorting sidings it has route-selected. A teleprinter by the control desk has already reproduced the 'cut list' as the traffic clerk typed it and the control desk operator now makes a quick check between his illuminated panel and the teleprint's first four entries; if there should be any discrepancy he can use the desk push buttons to cancel the incorrect route-setting and interpose the correct one. This is rarely necessary, and the next step is to order humping to begin.

Two operators normally man the Control Room and by now one of them will have summoned up a diesel-electric shunting locomotive to the rear of the train to be sorted. For Margam duty

CARS GO BY RAIL

Right: More and more motorcars travel by rail nowadays – either new from manufacturer to distributor in order to eliminate wear and damage during delivery; or, in private ownership, to eliminate the strain of long-distance driving. British Railways pioneered the 'Car-Sleeper' train, of which the Perth-London service is seen soon after beginning its journey from Scotland behind Class 'A1' 4-6-2 No. 60161 *North British*; the cars travel in single-deck, covered vans at the front of the train, the motorists and their passengers in sleeping cars at the rear.

[W. J. V. Anderson

Left: The more generous clearances of the Continent allow the German Federal Railway to build massive double-deck covered car transporters, of which one is seen here in Switzerland. Cars are driven on through a wide centre door (*below inset*) on a swivelling platform, from which they can be moved to a lower deck position, or which can be raised bodily to give access to the upper deck.

[G. M. Kichenside

Below left: A double-deck car transporter employed by British Railways, which incorporates a lift in the centre by which cars can be dropped to the lower deck. A covered version of this vehicle is being introduced on East Coast car-carrying trains for private motorists.

Below right: A double-deck car-carrier on the French National Railways; it has room in the centre of the decks for two small cars side by side.

a number of these machines have been equipped with two-way radio telephone, so that the driver will have received his order over his cab loudspeaker. In addition, the cab of each diesel shunter displays a replica of the signal at the crest of the hump, to keep the driver continually advised of the speed at which he is required to propel his train at times when the signal itself may be obscured from his view; the cab repeater is operated by coded frequency current signals through the running rails, which are picked up by inductor coils on the locomotive.

The French, incidentally, have taken this radio control much farther by experimenting with remote operation, from the Control Tower, of a crewless 650 h.p. diesel-electric bogie locomotive employed on hump operation at their yard at Achères. The radio control apparatus permits speed, braking and reversing to be accurately governed with perfect smoothness.

At Margam, the Control Tower operator begins the humping operation by clearing the humping signal and pushing a 'start tape' button on his desk. In the Traffic Office below, the tape begins to pass through the reader, which sets the electronic route-setting apparatus in action. As the first cut rolls down from the hump, it follows the first route on the tape, which is already picked out in white lights on the control desk diagram; but as the cut occupies each track circuit these white lights change to red. When it has passed the 'King' points – as the first fork below the hump of a marshalling yard is always known; naturally enough, the points further sub-dividing each arm of the fork are the 'Queens', and the next set, the 'Jacks' – the Traffic Office tape-reader automatically moves on to the next entry and begins to set up the correct route for the second 'cut', proceeding a step at a time until it detects from the track circuit occupation that the first one is safely out of the path required by its successor. Up on the Control Room desk, the illuminated indications of the sidings to which the 'cuts' are being routed step up in correspondence; and soon the second 'cut' is rolling down into the correct siding, while a third is poised on the hump ready to follow it. The process continues, entirely automatically, until the complete train has been sorted, without the humping diesel having to pause for a second in its slow but steady propulsion of the wagons over the hump.

It would not do, however, for the wagons to be left to make their own pace into the sidings, possibly to cannon destructively into others already there. In the old days yards had to employ squads of 'chasers' to scurry alongside each 'cut' and drop the wagon handbrakes with a cumbersome shunting pole at the critical moment. Now the 'cuts' are braked by electronically controlled retarders, which are air-operated beams that rise up to grip the wagons' wheel-rims at varying pressures. At Margam each 'cut' has to pass through two retarders in succession on its descent from the hump.

The retarders should brake a 'cut' sufficiently for it to reach the last wagons previously humped into the siding for which it is destined; but the meeting must be at slow speed – not more than walking pace. It follows that to achieve this the electronic controls of the retarder must know a great deal about the 'cut' – its weight; its 'rollability' or, in other words, whether it is stiff in the axleboxes, a medium-, or a free-runner; the siding to which it is going, for some will have a straight approach, others an entry of varying curvature which will act as a brake; and, not least, how far it has to run in its appointed siding before it meets wagons already occupying that track. All this data is fed to the computers controlling the retarders in respect of each cut.

The first set of retarders below the hump – the primaries – is concerned chiefly with keeping each 'cut' a safe distance in rear of its predecessor. Weight and rollability are therefore the factors principally governing the braking pressure they exert. Inductive wheel detectors in advance of the retarders, working with a high-speed electronic counter, calculate the acceleration rate of the 'cut' and thus its rollability; and the other information is provided by weight detectors. When the primary retarders have finished with this data it is passed on automatically to the secondary retarders.

By each retarder there are at track level radar eyes, beamed on to the approaching 'cut'. From the time in which the radar beams are reflected, the apparatus assesses the actual speed of the cut at any given second. Other detecting devices take note of the track circuit occupation in each siding and hence how many wagons each track is holding. The computer therefore takes note of the selected siding and absorbs a factor for its curvature: makes allowance for the number of wagons already standing on that track and thus the distance the 'cut' has to run: deduces the desirable speed of the 'cut' in the light of this information: measures that speed against the

The 'Flecha del Sur' of the Chilean State Railways runs the 675 miles between Santiago and Puerto Montt, travelling down the central valley of Chile between the coastal mountains and the Andes. It is hauled by an American-built General Electric 1,600 h.p. diesel-electric locomotive

[Blocks courtesy of J. Stone & Co. (Deptford) Ltd.

The 'Khyber Mail' of Pakistan's North Western Railway, seen passing through the yards of Lahore, provides a daily service for travellers on the Karachi–Lahore–Rawalpindi–Peshawar route, a distance of 1,045 miles. Its de luxe accommodation includes a sleeping car and dining car, and these two vehicles are fully air-conditioned by Stone-Carrier equipment. The diesel locomotive is U.S.-built.

The Dowty automatic coupler, which is being tested by British Railways. It will engage and lock under a wide range of track curvature and gradient conditions, simultaneously connecting the vacuum brake-pipes as well as making a traction link. It is compatible with all previous British Railways types of wagon coupling, though not with the Buckeye coupler used on coaching stock.

actual pace of the 'cut' as recorded by the radar eyes: and then applies braking pressure sufficient to eliminate the difference between these two speeds. The outcome should be a buffering-up in the siding at a comfortable speed of 4 m.p.h.

This careful judgment of the speed of meeting in the sidings may one day have more point that it has now at Margam. In the U.S.A., for example, freight cars are fitted with an automatic coupling that incorporates self-sealing brake connections and the speed of wagon release from automated yard retarders is regulated to ensure correct engagement when the cars kiss couplers. The U.S.S.R. is another country with an automatic device of this kind; and at the time of writing the West European railways are trying to agree amongst themselves on a fully automatic coupler for standardization throughout the Continent, where international through freight working steadily increases (the latest development is a freight version of the 'Trans-Europe-Express' scheme, known as 'Trans-Europ Express Marchandises', or 'T.E.E.M.').

British Railways have baulked at the cost of a fully automatic coupler which, with the installation of continuous brakes, adds 50 per cent to the price of a four-wheeled mineral wagon, although they have already tested some devices of this character. Only if each wagon is able to earn more – that is, by seeing more use through an increase of block train working, so that it wastes less time in yards; or by carrying more – will an automatic coupler of any kind so far tested be an economical proposition. But, as we have already observed, there are practical objections to an increase in wagon capacity. Without an automatic coupler, unfortunately, there can be little or no equipment of B.R. mineral wagons with continuous brakes, for those who handle these vehicles on private industrial premises, as well as railway staff, object to bobbing under the buffers of wagons to couple up brakepipe hoses; moreover, the connection of brake-pipes in B.R. marshalling yards protracts train assembly and means that the speed gained by the electronic devices just described is wasted because it takes longer to clear the sidings of sorted trains. There is an additional problem in that the present vacuum brake fittings underneath a mineral wagon foul many tippling devices for rapid unloading in industrial premises up and down the country, although the use of disc brakes, with which British Railways are experimenting on freight vehicles at the time of writing, may eradicate this difficulty. But it is the high cost of a fully automatic coupler which makes its widespread application in Britain – and in most other European countries – increasingly unlikely in the near future.

VIII

THE ELECTRONIC AGE OF SIGNALLING

AN express for London, headed by one of British Railways' latest blue-liveried 25 kV a.c. electric locomotives, is leaving Manchester Piccadilly. This is the London Road station that was rebuilt and re-styled from the platform to the ceiling of its great roof arches in order to match the new trains. Just outside it, on the west side of the approach tracks, stands a massive rectangular building with deep, wide windows. Here, in one of the three intricate all-electric signal-boxes which now control most of the 40-odd route miles of main line between Manchester and Crewe, electronics are going to work to see the London train safely on its way with the minimum of human intervention.

The rear wall of the operating floor of the signalbox is completely occupied by the wide sweep of a control console. Above this is framed an illuminated diagram of the track layout from the platforms of Manchester Piccadilly to Slade Lane Junction, 2.3 miles away, where the main line to Crewe, the South and the West divides into routes via Stockport and via Styal, which are reunited at Wilmslow. The whole of this complicated trackwork, which includes the divergence of the former L.N.E.R. route to Penistone and Sheffield, is under the control of the three signalmen at the console. They are supervised by a Traffic Regulator who sits at a desk at the front of the room, by the windows, from which he can command the complete extent of the illuminated diagram.

Taking a closer look at the illuminated diagram, you will see that the path being followed by our London train is lit up in white lights from one end to the other. In this way the signalmen have at any moment a reminder of the routes they have set up through the layout. They have evidence of the train's position, too, in the pairs of red lights which, one pair at a time, are lighting, then being extinguished as the next pair is illuminated along the row of white lights. These red lights show the occupation in sequence of each track circuit as the train makes its way up the selected path.

Track circuiting is one of the fundamentals of modern signalling. The two running rails are made to conduct a low current between a battery and a relay and they are insulated into sections, the lengths of which depend on the character of the signalling and the line. The current's normal path is through the rails and the relay coil, but the wheels and axles of a passing train short-circuit it, releasing the relay. The resulting change in the flow of the current is used for a variety of purposes in modern signalling. First and foremost, it is employed for safety, to actuate locks that prevent signals being cleared behind, or the points and signals being mistakenly altered in, or in front of, an occupied track circuit – in other words, its main purpose is to protect the path on each side of a train. As an extension of this idea, it can be used for automatic signalling, reverting signals to danger behind an occupied track circuit, then clearing them at a safe margin in rear of a train.

Amongst its other functions, track circuiting is now being used in Britain, as it has been for some time on the Continent, to operate road level-crossing barriers automatically; thereby signalmen are relieved of the job of opening and shutting gates, as well as attending to their signalling instruments, or else signalboxes or crossing-keepers installed purely to protect the crossing are being abolished, which saves the railways money. At a suitable distance from the crossing for a safety margin of time there is a track circuit which, when it is occupied by an oncoming train, causes warning lights beamed on the road approaches to flash (in some cases a two-tone gong rings to emphasize the warning) and then the barriers begin to lower. When the train has cleared the crossing, its occupation of another selected track circuit raises the barrier again, reopening the road for traffic.

A typical European automatically-operated, half-barrier level crossing. This one is on the French Railways. The barriers are raised and lowered in accordance with the passage of the trains, which actuate the level crossing equipment through the track circuiting, as described in this chapter.

Track circuiting also indicates the presence of trains to signalmen. We have already mentioned the red lights on the Manchester Piccadilly signalbox diagram, which denote the track circuit our London-bound train is occupying at any given moment. Close by the site of each running signal on the diagram is a small panel; and these small panels report the movement of our train – again, by courtesy of the track circuiting – in more detailed fashion. The panel nearest to the track circuit now occupied by our express is showing, in small illuminated figures and a letter, a four-character code. Soon the lights go out, but the same code is lit up in the next panel

Inside the operating room of Manchester Piccadilly signalbox. On the left is the traffic regulator's desk, overlooking the illuminated route diagram and the operating console, a portion of which is seen in the right-hand picture. The panels in which the four-character train descriptions appear can be discerned at various points on the illuminated route diagram above the console.

[*British Railways*

along the line the train is taking; and so it goes on, with the code moving from panel to panel in step with the train's actual progress from signal to signal on the track towards Slade Lane Junction, until it reaches the far end of the diagram, where it finally disappears. But now it begins a similar march across the illuminated diagram of Wilmslow cabin, if the train is running via Styal to Crewe.

The code, which identifies precisely each train to all signalmen and railway operating staff, is being adopted on most of British Railways because today's electronic science can make such valuable use of it in signalling apparatus. Every new diesel and electric locomotive or multiple-unit is fitted to display the code of the train it is hauling, instead of the headlamps of steam days

The British Railways four-character train description headcode is clearly seen on the front of the locomotive in this view of the northbound Euston–Glasgow 'Caledonian', train No. 1S83. Headed by English Electric Type '4' diesel locomotive No. D336, it is approaching Harrow.

[M. Edwards

(but the headlamp code will have to be used on many trains for some time yet until every traction unit has the means of displaying the four-character code). How the codes are made up is described in the panel on page 133. The code of each train is shown against it in the Regional working timetables – the railwaymen's own timetables, which print a great deal more information about passenger trains than the public books and timesheets, and which show all regularly scheduled goods trains – and is used to refer to the train in any special working notices, telegrams or telephone messages. This, coupled with the appearance of the same code on the signal-box diagram *and* on the front of the train itself, enormously assists operating staff.

132

THE FOUR-CHARACTER BRITISH RAILWAYS HEADCODE SYSTEM

British Railways are replacing the headlamp code for their trains with a new four-character code, which ultimately every train will display throughout its journey as a positive indication of its identity. As explained in the accompanying chapter, the codes are also used in modern signalbox train describer systems and to identify the trains in the working timetables, extra traffic notices and other documents or telephone messages concerning train running.

The first character in each code is a numeral which indicates the class of train in accordance with the standard British Railways signalbox bell-code system and the previous headlamp code, as follows:

Description	Class of Train	Signal-box Bell Code	First Number of Headcode
Express passenger train	A	4	1
Newspaper train	A	4	1
Ordinary passenger train	B	3–1	2
Mixed train	B	3–1	2
Branch passenger train	B	1–3	2
Parcels train	C	1–3–1	3
Livestock or perishable train composed entirely of vehicles conforming to coaching stock requirements	C	1–3–1	3
Empty coaching stock train	C	2–2–1	3
Express freight, livestock or perishable train, with the automatic brake operative on not less than:			
75 per cent of the vehicles	C	3–1–1	4
One-third of the vehicles	D	5	5
4 vehicles	E	1–2–2	6
not fitted with continuous brake, but with limited load	E	1–2–2	6
not fitted with continuous brake	F	3–2	7
Mineral or ballast train	J	4–1	9
Through freight mineral or ballast train	H	1–4	8
Freight, mineral or ballast train stopping at intermediate stations	K	3	9
Branch freight train	K	1–2	9
Light engine or engines	G	2–3	0
Light engine and brakevan	G	1–1–3	0

In general, except for local freight trains and light engines, the second character of the headcode, which is a letter, identifies the destination area of the train or, in the case of local working, the area in which it runs. This is how the letters are used on the Western Lines of the London Midland Region:

Terminating Area	Letter	Terminating Area	Letter
Trains local to the L.M.R.		*Trains local to the L.M.R.*	
Euston	A	Blackpool and Fylde ⎫	
Euston and Rugby	B	Derby ⎬	P
St. Pancras ⎫		Excursion and Special ⎭	
Marylebone ⎬	C	trains local to L.M.R. *	
Nottingham ⎫		*Inter-Regional Trains*	
Chester ⎬	D	To Eastern Region	E
Leicester	F	To London Midland Region	M
Birmingham	G	To North Eastern Region	N
Manchester South and Stoke	H	To Southern Region	O
Manchester North	J	To Scottish Region	S
Liverpool Lime Street and Crewe ⎫		To Western Region	V
Liverpool Central ⎬	K	Inter-Regional Excursion ⎫	
Barrow, Preston and Carlisle ⎭	L	and Special trains ⎭	X

* For freight trains, 'T' indicates trip train.

The third and fourth characters of each headcode are numerals. In general, these denote the individual number of the train in the class and on the route specified by the first two characters of the code. Thus on the Western Region train 1B11 is an express passenger ('1') from Paddington to Weston-super-Mare ('B' identifying the Bristol area as its destination) leaving at 1.15 p.m. ('11', the third and fourth characters, specifying the particular train among those between Paddington and Weston-super-Mare).

As our train was about to leave Manchester Piccadilly the signalman there set up its code by depressing the appropriate buttons in a numbered and lettered group on his console (on the Western Region, the signalmen do this by fingering a telephone-type dial). The Styal route to Crewe is controlled entirely by signalboxes of the same kind as Manchester Piccadilly; the other two are at Wilmslow and Sandbach and govern 27 route miles of main line between them. These two cabins have nothing to do with the headcode description of Manchester–Crewe through trains on their illuminated diagrams. Once the correct code has been set up and transmitted at Manchester Piccadilly it steps forward automatically, not only the length of the illuminated diagram in that cabin, but then from that cabin to the Wilmslow cabin diagram; after traversing Wilmslow territory from end to end, the code jumps on in time with the train to the first panel of the Sandbach cabin diagram; and from the last panel by a running signal on the Sandbach diagram the code is passed in due course to Crewe North box. Should our train have to be side-tracked *en route* to allow a following train to get in front, the electronic apparatus will take note and sidetrack its code with it, passing the correct code of the overtaking trains up the main line ahead of the one that has been delayed. The same process operates with trains in the reverse direction, of course; and if the signalmen at Wilmslow or Sandbach have a train starting or terminating in their bailiwick, then they have the means to originate or cancel a headcode description accordingly. At the time of writing there is a gap in these modern signalling arrangements on the other Manchester–Crewe route via Stockport, but in due course a new cabin in the Stockport area will fill it; and ultimately automatic train describer apparatus will function from end to end of the Euston–Crewe–Manchester and Liverpool main lines.

There are other purposes to which these train descriptions can be put in modern signalling, though as yet not on British main lines. Several of the latest all-electric signalling installations at major German Federal Railway traffic centres incorporate automatic train describer apparatus. The most complex of them is in the cabin which towers above the approaches to the main station at Frankfurt-am-Main and controls not only its 24 platforms, into which eight routes converge in a wide stream of running lines, but a complicated network of avoiding lines surrounding the city. Frankfurt is the busiest station in Western Germany and the cabin signals over 2,000 trains a day, 1,250 of them into or out of the station, where the daily total of all train, empty stock, light engine and shunting movements is between 4,000 and 5,000.

In their new, power-operated signalboxes covering a big and complicated area of trackwork, like Manchester Piccadilly, British Railways are making special provision for Traffic Regulators, who like generals in battle sit at the rear, watching that detail activity by the signalmen on each sector of the console is co-ordinated to achieve smooth progress over the whole front. In German signalling practice the Traffic Controller at major traffic centres has an even more commanding role in the signalbox and dictates routing instructions for every train into and out of the station to his signalmen. In the very busy Frankfurt cabin there are two Traffic Controllers, controlling five signalmen, each sitting at an individual switch console covering a portion of the station layout. At the back of the operating floor is a wide diagram of the rail network surrounding the city. To allow the Traffic Controllers to devote most of their time to the broad strategic picture of traffic working, a great deal of the route-setting on this diagram at the rear of the room is automatic; at several outlying junctions the trains set their own routes, the apparatus detecting which path they wish to take from their descriptive code numbers, one character of which symbolizes a specific route.

I have myself seen this device demonstrated in the Frankfurt cabin. I watched as an express from Mainz neared the city and its descriptive routing code letter and train number were lit up in a panel at the left-hand end of the big wall diagram at the back of the box. As the train penetrated closer to the station, signal repeater lights on the diagram changed from red to green and the train's letter and number moved inward from track circuit to track circuit. Then, for the sake of our demonstration, one of the operators deliberately stepped in and took over from the automatic controls, as he can for any abnormal movement in everyday conditions, to set up a wrong route at one of the automatic junctions ahead of the incoming train. Lights began to flash at the appropriate spot on the diagram to indicate that the route at that junction was no longer set normal. Then, sure enough, when the moving red lights and the progress of its description from panel to panel showed the train to be only two track circuits away from the

WONDER SIGNALBOX AT FRANKFURT

This imposing signalbox at Frankfurt–am–Main, Western Germany, controls not only one of Western Europe's busiest stations, but also a wide area of surrounding rail territory. The extent of that territory can be guessed from the two pictures ((*centre left and right*) showing the illuminated diagram of the approach area at the rear of the operating floor, with the controlling signalman seated in front of it (the lady in the left-hand picture is the Frankfurt station announcer). Notice the simplicity of the operators' control desks, possible because several of the outlying junctions are operated automatically by the trains themselves, as described in the accompanying chapter. The bottom pictures show the other end of the operating floor, with the station area supervisors who give instructions to the signalmen at the individual route-setting desks (*bottom left*); and a close-up of one of the five signalling desks among which the station operation is divided (*bottom right*). Here again the panels on which the illuminated train descriptions are displayed can be clearly discerned on the layout diagram.

[*German Federal Railway*

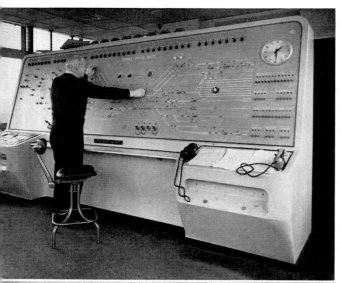

Left: Two of the compact types of signalbox console now employed by British Railways. In each case the control of signals and points on the layout is by route-setting thumb switches at the appropriate places on the illuminated layout diagram. The upper picture shows the console in Temple Mills East signalbox, in the London area of the Eastern Region; the lower one shows the console of Plymouth signalbox, Western Region, which incorporates an additional layout diagram above the operating console to display the four-character train descriptions.

[British Railways

Above: Two types of route indicator used in association with colour-light signals by British Railways – the 'theatre' type (upper), in which a descriptive number or letter appropriate to the route is displayed in lights; and the directional type (lower), which advises drivers of a diverging route by a line of lunar-white lights at the appropriate angle.

[British Railways

MODERN SIGNALLING ON BRITISH RAILWAYS

Below: Two pictures which underline the economy and clarity of modern colour-light signalling. The left-hand picture shows the complicated gantry which originally controlled the approach of the London Midland main line to Rugby and the right-hand picture the three colour-light signals with associated route indicators which have replaced it, and which convey all the necessary route indications.

[W. S. Garth, P. Ransome-Wallis

automatic junction, the routing code letter in its description did its job; the lights stopped flashing and the junction reset itself correctly to suit the train's requirements.

The simultaneous advances in colour-light signalling and in the application of electric or compressed air power to the operation of signal and point mechanisms during this century have made obsolescent the wayside signalbox, controlling an area limited by the distance at which semaphore signals and points could be efficiently worked by wires and rodding. On the open main line the need for intermediate signalboxes is reduced because of automatic colour-light signalling, worked safely by the trains themselves through the track circuits. Where the main line is intersected by junctions it is now practical to control them and even whole branch lines remotely, so that the trend today is to centralize signalling in a small number of superbly equipped boxes, each of which, thanks to electronics, performs the work it took several times as many of the old mechanical signal cabins to do. The Manchester Piccadilly box, for example, has absorbed the functions of 13 signal cabins of the old kind, which had no fewer than 858 levers between them. Apart from anything else, this centralization of signalling substantially accelerates the traffic, particularly freight, because movements through a complex layout can be conceived with an eye to the situation throughout the area, whereas previously each of the many signalboxes could get the overall picture only by elaborate consultation with their neighbours or with a central Control Office.

Colour-light signals themselves are also an asset to swifter train running, partly because their aspects are clearly identified from much greater distances than semaphores, especially in the worst weather conditions, and partly because they are much more conveniently adapted to show a number of differing aspects. The advantage of this last characteristic is that enginemen can be given a more precise indication of the state of the road ahead of them and can therefore adjust their speed more accurately to the traffic conditions in which they find themselves. Most present-day British Railways colour-light signalling schemes use four aspects – red, yellow, double-yellow and green – for running signals. A yellow aspect warns a driver that he must be prepared to stop at a red aspect at the next running signal; a double-yellow aspect gives him earlier warning of the red aspect and precedes the single yellow. Running through a sequence of yellows, a driver will soon realize that he is following another train. If there were only a single yellow, he would have to apply his brake fully in case he should find his next signal at red; but the earlier warning of the double yellow allows him a margin to control his speed until he can see by the succession of double yellows he is getting that it matches that of the train in front of him. If his adjustment has been successfully guessed, he may have only to touch his brake from time to time until he has been routed past the offending train ahead. Obviously, this results in a smoother flow of traffic on heavily occupied sections of track.

In a complex layout such as Manchester Piccadilly many subsidiary signals are employed to permit limited shunting or other movements that can be carried out without having to clear the whole of the territory protected by a main running signal, or to govern activity on non-running lines. For these purposes a ground-level position-light signal is generally preferred nowadays to the miniature colour-light or semaphore-type disc; the position-light signal has three lights arranged triangularly, the bottom left red and the other two white, and is at danger when the red and the right-hand white lights are illuminated, clear when both white lights are showing. In some shunting signals the bottom left-hand light is yellow instead of red, to indicate that it may be passed at danger in certain circumstances.

In days of old drivers were warned of a facing junction ahead and which line they were to take at it by a profusion of semaphore signals, one for each possible routing. Now one colour-light signal, supplemented by a route indicator, suffices. Above the signal aspects three lunar-white lights are mounted for each possible divergence from the main line and these are angled to each other to indicate the respective routes to which they refer; if the junction is set for one of the diverging lines, the appropriate set of three white lights on the route indicator is illuminated. It would be practically impossible to use this device to indicate to a driver approaching Manchester Piccadilly which of its many platforms was waiting to accept his train; in a situation like this, the signal protecting entry to the station is equipped with a route indicator showing in white lights the number or code letter of the track to be followed.

The modern signalman does not have to have a separate control for each pair of points,

The economy of modern signalling is apparent also in this view of the south end of York station, British Railways. Shunting movements over the complicated layout are fully protected by the neat position-light ground signals, all under the control of York's central, power-operated signal cabin.

[*British Railways*

running signal, subsidiary signal or route indicator. In normal circumstances he does his work with route-setting switches, each of which will set up the full extent of a route protected by an individual signal; there will be controls on his console, so that he can alter each pair of points independently if desired, but he will only use these in an emergency. If the signal has a route indicator, this will automatically display the correct trio of lights or number according to the way he has moved his route switches.

In the latest British Railways power-signalling cabins two kinds of console are used. At Manchester Piccadilly, Wilmslow and Sandbach, the illuminated diagram and the route-setting switches are separated. The latter are neatly grouped on the console below the diagram and numbered to correspond with the key references of the signals on the layout; the switches governing running signals are coloured red and those actuating subsidiary signals are white. Little red and green repeater lights above each switch remind the signalmen at any moment of the aspects the signals are displaying to drivers. When the signalman moves a switch to reset a route, the intricate electronic apparatus in the lower floor of the cabin first tests all the routes that could conflict with the one selected and satisfies itself that they are not set to do so; it also proves that all the track circuits protected by the signal to be cleared are in fact unoccupied; then it moves the points as required and checks that they have gone home correctly; and finally it clears the signal. As soon as the train has vacated the track circuits protected by the signal, the latter will automatically revert to danger without any action on the signalman's part. Some of the thumb-switches for running signals are three-position; the third position enables the signalman to set these signals for fully automatic operation, if the traffic conditions are suitable for it.

A neater arrangement that is used in some of the other power-operated modern signal-boxes the London Midland Region is installing – at Edge Hill, Liverpool, for example – and which is found in several recent cabins on other Regions, combines illuminated diagram and controls in one console. The diagram forms the operating desk and the controls and repeater lights are located in exact geographical relation to the signals they govern. Some console designs of this kind use 'entrance-exit,' or 'NX', push-button controls; to set a route through the layout, the signalman presses a button on the diagram at its commencement and another at its conclusion.

One of the most valuable contributions electronic science has made to the signal engineer is the coded impulse system of control. No longer is it necessary to carry a separate cable from every signalbox switch to the respective recipients of their commands – the points and the signals on the ground. The electrical impulses to a large group of apparatus can be conveyed on the same wire, each impulse being coded to actuate a particular point or signal. The outcome is that it has become possible to control as much as 100 route miles of track from one signalbox without extravagant expenditure on the provision and maintenance of innumerable control cables. Centralized Traffic Control, or C.T.C., is the phrase by which the various methods embodying the principles I have outlined are known on most railways.

C.T.C. is just beginning to feature in British Railways' modernization schemes. By C.T.C. methods Manchester Piccadilly signalbox remotely controls the vital Slade Lane Junction and the suburban station layouts at Mauldeth Road and Didsbury. Sandbach and Wilmslow similarly take charge of intermediate station layouts some distance from them. On the Southern Region, the whole of the Sheerness-on-Sea branch is remotely operated from the all-electric signalbox at the Kent Coast main-line junction of Sittingbourne. These are limited applications of the idea, however, compared with some abroad on less heavily-trafficked lines where it is practicable to put far greater mileages of route under the supervision of a single control centre.

Sweden boasts the most extensive C.T.C. installation in Europe. In the southern half of the country a privately-operated electric railway runs 186 miles, single track throughout except for passing loops, from an inland mining area to the Baltic port of Oxelösund, south of Stockholm, and carries a substantial iron-ore traffic and some passenger railcar services amounting to 30 trains each way daily. The whole of this railway, with its 36 intermediate stations, 280 pairs of points and 335 signals, can be controlled from one post at Skogstorp by C.T.C., although the intermediate stations have control panels capable of independent operation by the local staff for shunting operations if the Skogstorp control centre releases these panels electrically. The signalling between stations on this railway is automatic; but in addition to the other signals and points which require control, the Skogstorp headquarters remotely operates some station level-crossing barriers, three swing bridges over waterways and such incidental apparatus as point

The C.T.C. installation at Skogstorp, in Sweden, described in the accompanying chapter, from which 186 miles of a single-track route are fully controlled. The passage of trains throughout the route is automatically recorded on the moving graphs in the foreground.

heaters – a highly essential item for winter working in these latitudes – which the C.T.C. operator can switch on at a suitable interval before he requires to move points, so as to be sure they will not be frozen and unresponsive to the electrical controls.

All this means that the control cables from the Skogstorp panel must be capable of conveying some 850 different coded impulses outward and 3,600 inward. The inward impulses confirm on indicator lights the correct functioning of the apparatus miles away on the ground and the progress of the trains. This is shown both in lights on an illuminated layout diagram and recorded automatically by pens on moving graphs to form a lasting record of a day's working. All these coded controls are conveyed out and back on only six channels, which in a normal 24 hours' working carry as many as 100,000 different commands between the control panel and the signals, points and other equipment. Devices of this kind are expensive to install but before long they are amply repaying the investment through staff reduction and more efficient working.

C.T.C., although it is now spreading throughout the globe, has so far been most widely developed in the U.S.A. There it was the natural development, using modern electronic science, of the dispatcher method of train control practised on the long stretches of single track main line common in sparsely populated areas of that great country. In operating conditions of this sort, and with trains usually sporadic, it was never practical to provide signalling as we know it in Britain, and traffic was regulated by dispatchers at strategic points; they were in communication with each other and kept drivers informed of any local amendment to the time-table – for example, of an alteration of passing arrangements at a loop normally scheduled to one farther on, because a train was running behind schedule. This system still prevails widely in the U.S.A. – and, incidentally, on the fast-developing railways of the U.S.S.R. – but it is increasingly giving place to C.T.C.

On a larger scale, C.T.C. enables valuable economies in the provision of multiple tracks and their maintenance. Where traffic moves in well-defined directional peaks, it is often the case that two or more tracks, essential to cope with it at its heaviest, are wasted when it is at its lowest. The ideal is a track (or tracks) that can be signalled and connected to the other running lines suitably for use in either direction, so that it can be brought into play either way according to need. To make the best use of such a bi-directional track, it is essential that its controller has the widest view of the traffic situation on his main line, for he must obviously avoid having trains seeking entry to his bi-directional section from both ends.

The economies possible through reduction of track maintenance and other associated costs induced the New York Central to embark on a £15 million scheme to narrow the world's longest stretch of four tracks – $473\frac{3}{4}$ miles almost unbroken on its New York–Chicago main line – to two and control them from several C.T.C. panels. The first section to be modified, the 163 miles between Buffalo and Cleveland, is now controlled entirely by two men in a C.T.C. office at Erie, nearly half-way. Both remaining lines are signalled for reversible working and connected by crossovers at roughly 6-mile intervals which can be negotiated at 50 m.p.h. Using two of these crossovers, for example, the C.T.C. operators can seize a lull in the traffic one way to loop a slow-moving freight going the other way on to the adjacent line and allow an express behind it to speed clear, whereafter the freight will be switched back on to its original track at the next crossover.

British Railways have scheduled one or two more modest applications of the same principles (on our main lines the directional peaks are not clearly enough defined to make the New York Central methods practicable). The Central Wales line from Craven Arms to Llandovery is being developed as a relief route for the ever-growing freight traffic between South Wales and the north, but the Western Region feels it can be more efficiently operated and its capacity in fact increased by converting it throughout to single track with passing loops, closing 18 signal-boxes and operating the entire 60 route miles by C.T.C. from a cabin at Llandrindod Wells. The North Eastern Region is likewise preparing to single its York–Hull line as far as Beverley and control the singled section entirely from York by C.T.C.

The French have already marched a step farther – to automatic C.T.C. on a $27\frac{1}{2}$-mile section of their line from Dôle to Vallorbe, one of the important links with Switzerland in the South-East Region of the French National Railways. When C.T.C. was installed, this section was reduced from double to single track, with passing loops at three intermediate stations. As a

Programme machines on London Transport (see page 142) – the main picture shows the supervisory control room of the Northern Line at Leicester Square, with repeaters of the controlling programme machines visible in screens on the right; the inset is a close-up of a programme machine, with the feelers which read the punched information on each working at the base of the instrument.

[London Transport

train approaches one of these passing loops, it occupies a track circuit which activates electronic apparatus that will signal the train safely through the station.

In his control room, the C.T.C. operator for this section can pre-set successively the routes through all three stations for up to four trains – and they need not all be going the same way over the single line. His apparatus will 'store' all these route-settings in its electronic memory, reminding the operator of his selections by displaying them – with, in each case, the direction of running he has ordered – on illuminated panels above the switch console, a panel for each station. When the first train of the four occupies the key track circuit outside a station, the illuminated route selections for that station on the operator's panel step down one, to show the operator that the route he has pre-set is now being correctly set up; and out on the track, the train concerned is now signalled to run straight through, to overtake a preceding train on the loop, or to pass one coming the other way, as the case may be. As soon as the train has cleared the station, the route selection for it at this passing place is extinguished on the operator's panel, and on the track the points and signals at the station are automatically restored to normal – or reset to permit the departure of a train that has been passed or overtaken there, as soon as the line is clear. Similarly, the second train of the four signals itself according to its pre-set route at each station; so do the third and the fourth. The point of this ingenious apparatus will be fully realized when in due course the control panel is transferred to a corner of the big traffic control-room at Dijon. There, as at Frankfurt, with its automatically-operated junctions, this development of C.T.C. will undoubtedly enable Traffic Controllers to supervise a wider area strategically without having to absorb themselves in the minute-by-minute signalling detail of trains on this section of the Dôle–Vallorbe single line.

Can automatic signalling be developed further still – even to the completely automated operation of the trains themselves? Only a decade ago robot passenger trains would have been considered a fairly wild dream (though the General Post Office has a robot underground railway beneath the streets of London, to ferry mails between its Mount Pleasant sorting office and some London main-line termini). It is no longer a fantasy. In France, Germany, the U.S.A. and the U.S.S.R. there have already been successful experiments in the radio control of locomotives, and New York, San Francisco and Hamburg seem to be vying to produce the world's first fully automatic suburban railway, with driverless trains, before the 1960s are out. (The San Francisco authorities, incidentally, have suggested that their trains should carry drivers for an initial period, even if these motormen have nothing to do, to reassure the passengers!) British readers need look no farther than London to see the basis of a fully automatic railway, for the in-town sections of London Transport's Northern Line are now signalled with scarcely any human intervention; and it is not difficult to imagine how the trains themselves could be automatically controlled by electronic means to conform with this signalling. The device employed by London Transport is known as a 'programme machine'; it was first installed on the Northern Line, and more refined versions have since been applied to the Metropolitan and Piccadilly systems.

The programme machine looks rather like the 'works' of an old-time player piano, or pianola. Running through it is a long sheet on which the train service has been set out as lines of tiny holes, punched at coded spaces to specify the timetable number, route and destination of each train. An electronic eye positions each line of holes accurately for them to be scanned by feelers, which actuate the signalling apparatus on the basis of what they learn. Each train itself – through the track circuiting, as usual – moves the sheet on to the next line when it has cleared the section controlled by the programme machine. But suppose a train is delayed en route and drops out of its timetable path? A time machine deals with contingencies of that sort. It is very similar to the programme machine, but its sheet moves on in strict accord with time and not with the trains – in other words, it functions as though the timetable were being worked with split-second accuracy. By intricate electronics there is no need to explore in detail, the time machine detects whether each train is on schedule and, if it should be late at a junction, 'thinks' the problem out with the programme machine to decide whether a train coming from another direction and running on time should be sent through the junction first and out of timetabled sequence; the machines will 'remember' to send on the late-running train in due course. The machines automatically warn the Northern Line's Central control-room at Leicester Square if the train running should get badly out of gear, so that the staff there can step in to take personal control of operations if they feel it necessary.

Most of the world's major railway systems now employ some form of cab signalling, to afford drivers and motormen an additional indication of the aspects of some, or all the signals along the routes they are travelling. These systems are usually reinforced by an automatic device that shuts off the power or applies the brakes, or both, if the driver or motorman neglects to act on an adverse aspect from a signal. The intention is not to relieve the engineman of his primary responsibility to keep watch on the road and signals ahead, but to make sure he has not missed the implications of a signal aspect – and especially to help him in conditions of poor visibility.

Over forty years ago the Great Western Railway introduced an Automatic Train Control system, which it was the first in this country to apply to the greater part of its system. The G.W.R. apparatus requires direct contact between a detector on the engine and a ramp laid between the running rails by each distant signal. For various reasons this was not deemed suitable for standardization throughout British Railways, who have developed an inductive method, known as the Automatic Warning System, or A.W.S., whereby the cab signalling effects are achieved through the interplay of electro-magnets and electrical currents. Means have now been devised to enable B.R. locomotives and multiple-units fitted with A.W.S. to detect both the ex-G.W. and B.R. track fittings (for the ex-G.W. methods have been retained by the Western Region), so that through motive power working between the Western Region and the rest of the British system will be possible with the cab signalling apparatus continually in use.

In the British Railways standard A.W.S. two adjacent magnets, the first permanent, the second an electro-magnet, are laid between the running rails some 200 yards in advance of each distant signal. Normally, with the distant signal at caution – and, in the case of colour-lights, this means the double as well as the single yellow aspect – the electro-magnet is dead. Each motive power unit carries a receiver below its front bufferbeam. The effect on this of the permanent magnet is to cause electrically a horn to sound in the cab. If the engineman takes no action, a brake application will begin automatically and become full within 10 or 20 seconds, according to the length of the train. Normally, of course, the engineman will be on the *qui vive* and make the appropriate acknowledgement, which is a touch of the resetting lever that enables him to take over control of the brakes himself. The warning horn also is silenced, but the engineman is not allowed to forget that he has now passed a distant signal at caution and that he must be on the alert for possible danger aspects. At eye-level in his cab a visual reminder device changes from an all-black to a conspicuous spoked black-and-yellow and stays thus until the next track permanent magnet at the next distant signal cancels the warning; but, should this distant signal be at caution too, the visual reminder will not have had time to resume its black aspect before the engine passes over the electro-magnet and the warning is reiterated. If the distant signal is clear, then the electro-magnet is energized. The effect of this on the motive power unit's receiver is to cancel the warning sequence initiated on its electrical circuits by the permanent magnet, before there has been time for the horn in the cab to sound or the brakes to be applied. All that happens now is that the engineman is reassured of the signal's clear aspect by a two-second ringing of a bell in his cab.

Most of the warning devices used by the world's major railways are inductive in operation. For example, half the German Federal Railway's main-line route mileage is equipped with the Indusi form of inductive automatic train control, the basis of which is interaction between magnets on the motive power unit and the track at different frequencies. The effect is that when a train passes a distant signal at caution, a track magnet applies the brakes unless the driver depresses a 'vigilance button' to indicate acknowledgment of the signal's warning. If he has

The apparatus of British Railways' standard Automatic Warning System, showing (*left*) the black-and-yellow spoked visual reminder device on the wall of a diesel locomotive cab; and (*right*) the receiver on Class 'A4' 4–6–2 No. 60007 *Sir Nigel Gresley* poised above a track magnet.

[*British Railways*

143

not reduced speed to at least 56 m.p.h. within 22 seconds of passing the adverse distant, or if he passes a second track magnet some 160 yards in advance of the home signal at more than 41 m.p.h., the apparatus will still apply the train brakes. Finally, a track magnet at the home signal, if the latter is on, will apply the brakes if the train overruns it. The system, which has been proved at train speeds of over 100 m.p.h., is designed to ensure that a stop signal at danger cannot be overrun by more than 220 yards in any circumstances, and German Federal track layouts are planned with this maximum safety overlap in mind.

Some systems provide the engineman with much more detailed information on the state of the road ahead than the British A.W.S. One of the most intricate is that of the Pennsylvania Railroad, U.S.A., which repeats accurately in the cab the aspects of the signals the driver is approaching. The 'Pennsy' employs position-light signalling, in which rows of white lights are illuminated vertically (clear), at an angle of 45 degrees (caution) or horizontally (danger); in places position-light signals are paired to increase the number of aspects and thereby inform the driver in advance of turnouts ahead and the speed to which he must reduce to negotiate them.

The 'Pennsy' track circuiting is coded. When a train passes a signal it shorts the circuit in the usual way, as we have already described, and a receiver connected to the track detects this. It now initiates a low-frequency coded impulse up the track to the next signal in rear, whose receiver counts the impulse, detects its meaning and alters the aspect of the signal to suit; it also sends an impulse at a different frequency up the track to the next signal, which is reset accordingly; and so the process goes on, until a high frequency passes through a track circuit that will begin fully to clear signals.

It is not only the signals which have their impulse counters. The locomotives, too, are fitted with detectors on their bogies, which count the impulse rate of every track circuit over which the train is travelling and repeat on miniature signals in the cab the exact aspects of the signals. Thus the engineman always has a clear picture in front of him of the signal aspect he is approaching, even if he cannot yet see the signal itself. A further development of these methods practised in the U.S.A. is that, where certain signal aspects require a driver to proceed at limited speed, the automatic warning devices will take control of the train's braking if he exceeds the prescribed maximum. In this, as in so many other ways, modern signalling, although it hands over more and more of human activity to electronic gadgetry, leaves less and less margin for errors that could prejudice safety. If a signalling device should fail, it is a cardinal rule that it must 'fail safe' – that is, if anything goes wrong, the immediate effect must be to bring trains to a stop. As a result, the railway the world over is still statistically by far the safest means of mechanical transport.

The best in modern railway station architecture is exemplified by these two views of the concourse and exterior of Rotterdam Central, in the Netherlands.

[Netherlands State Railways